THE ELEMENTS OF THE QABALAH

Will Parfitt has twenty years practical experience with esoteric psychology, the Tree of Life and the Qabalah. He has trained in Psychosynthesis and has had extensive experience of other therapies and techniques for spiritual and personal development, including neo-Reichian therapy. He has a private psychotherapy practice and runs seminars and workshops around the country on a variety of topics. His work focuses on inner harmony and the manifestation of purpose and creative potential. When not working, Will loves to dance and is a keen photographer. His other books from Element include *The Living Qabalah*, *Walking Through Walls*, and *The Elements of Psychosynthesis*.

The *Elements Of* is a series designed to present high quality introductions to a broad range of essential subjects.

The books are commissioned specifically from experts in their fields. They provide readable and often unique views of the various topics covered, and are therefore of interest both to those who have some knowledge of the subject, as well as those who are approaching it for the first time.

Many of these concise yet comprehensive books have practical suggestions and exercises which allow personal experience as well as theoretical understanding, and offer a valuable source of information on many important themes.

In the same series

Alchemy
The Arthurian Tradition
Astrology
Buddhism
The Celtic Tradition
The Chakras
Christian Symbolism
Creation Myth
The Druid Tradition
Dreamwork
Earth Mysteries
Feng Shui
The Goddess
The Grail Tradition
The Greek Tradition

Herbalism
Human Potential
Meditation
Mysticism
Natural Magic
Pendulum Dowsing
Prophecy
Psychosynthesis
Ritual Magic
Shamanism
Sufism
Tai Chi
Taoism
Visualisation

THE ELEMENTS OF

THE QABALAH

Will Parfitt

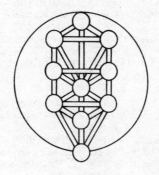

ELEMENT

Shaftesbury, Dorset ● Rockport, Massachusetts

Published in Great Britain in 1991 by
Element Books Limited
Longmead, Shaftesbury, Dorset

Published in the USA in 1991 by
Element Inc
42 Broadway, Rockport, MA 01966

Cover design and illustration by Max Fairbrother and Barbara McGavin
Typeset by Selectmove Ltd, London
Printed and bound in Great Britain by
Billings Ltd, Hylton Road, Worcester

British Library Cataloguing in Publication Data
Parfitt, Will
The elements of the Qabalah.
I. Title
135.4

Library of Congress Cataloging in Publication Data
Parfitt, Will.
The elements of the Qabalah / Will Parfitt.
Includes bibliographical references and index.
1. Capabla. I. Title II. Title: Qabalah.
BF1611.P35   1991
135′.4—dc20 91–30911

ISBN 1–85230–230–5

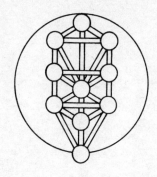

CONTENTS

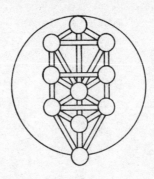

USING THIS BOOK

Each chapter of *The Elements of the Qabalah* contains the main text introducing the subject of that chapter followed by an exercise, which gives you the opportunity to connect with the Qabalah in an experiential way. The exercises are placed at the end of the chapter so that you can have greater choice as to how and when you practise them. You might like to do so immediately after reading the chapter, or you may prefer to leave them until you are feeling more in the mood. If you are reading this book whilst travelling, for example, you may prefer to wait until you are at home before attempting an exercise.

Before starting any of the exercises, ensure you have enough time to complete the exercise without being disturbed. Spend a few moments relaxing and centring yourself. Take up a comfortable position, either standing, sitting or lying as appropriate to the exercise, and with a straight but not stiff spine, close your eyes and take a few deep breaths. Be aware that you are a unique individual choosing at this time to perform this exercise. You are then ready to start the exercise. Take your time going through the instructions to the exercise – it is better to err on the side of slowness rather than rush things.

It may be necessary to read the exercise through a few times to familiarize yourself with what you have to do. This will help you to focus, so do not begrudge this time. If you find any particular exercise especially useful or meaningful to you, you can always repeat it more than once. Repetition of an exercise can, in fact, multiply its power in helping you realize more about yourself.

You might like to share the experience of the exercises with someone else, each of you alternately acting as guide and speaking the words and directions for the other person. If you do this, remember to respect the other person's process, and to speak slowly and distinctly, allowing him or her time to do whatever is required.

It is a good idea to keep a record of your work with the Tree of Life in a diary or workbook as, apart from anything else, it helps you to ground your experience. This simply means finding ways of expressing what you have learnt in your everyday life. The exercise at the end of Chapter 2 may make having a diary in which to record your Qabalistic work more real for you. Mostly, however, have fun with the exercises – taking a light approach can help you both connect with the work and keep a perspective on it.

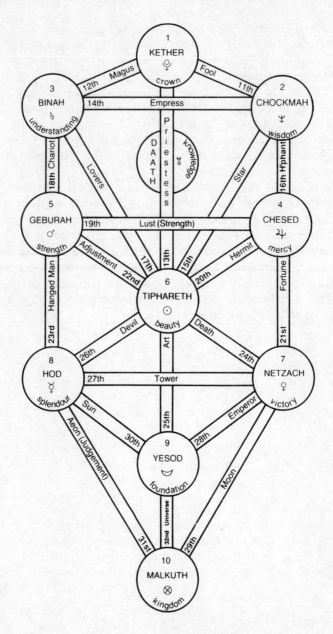

Diagram 1 The Tree of Life

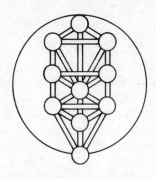

1 · WHAT IS THE QABALAH?

She is more precious than pearls; and all the things you value are not equal unto her. Length of days is in her right hand; in her left are riches and honour. Her ways are ways of pleasantness, and all her paths are peace. A tree of life is she to those that lay hold of her; and every one that firmly grasps her will be made happy.

King Solomon (*Book of Proverbs*)

The Qabalah, at the heart of the Western Mystery Tradition, is a way of personal development and self-realization based on a map of consciousness called the Tree of Life. It is a constant inspiration to seekers after inner wisdom, whatever their religion or belief. The Qabalah emphasizes the relevance of our ordinary, daily lives as an expression of our spirituality. It offers us a detailed, coherent world view, both of the nature of human existence and the relationship between ourselves, other beings, our planet and even the universe as a whole.

For many years the Qabalah appeared to be lost in obscurity, particularly in its practical applications, yet today, with so many people searching for spiritual roots, and looking for meaning and purpose in their lives, it is undergoing a remarkable come-back. Its influence has not only been in the spiritual realms, however, for it has also exerted a profound and lasting effect on the growth of modern Western Psychology. Although he kept it secret, we now know that Freud was interested in the Qabalah, and in his letters Jung made many knowledgeable references to the Tree of Life.

The Hebrew word Qabalah means 'to reveal', and it refers to the revelation of our own inner nature that can come from its study and use. The Qabalistic diagram known as the Tree of Life is a guide to the body, personality, soul and Spirit. It encompasses a philosophy and psychology of great theoretical and practical depth that deals with the whole person, not just the intellect, and it has been called 'the Mysticism of the West'.

The word Qabalah also means 'to receive', referring to our ability to receive inner wisdom and understanding. A distinction is made between 'knowledge', which is primarily theoretical, and 'understanding', which is primarily practical. Nothing can replace the experience of the Qabalah in its practical applications. To appreciate this fully, we have to engage all aspects of our being – our thinking, feeling and sensing functions – and not just the intellect.

The Qabalah can be divided into five parts. Firstly, there is the 'oral' Qabalah, aspects of the teaching received orally, either from a teacher of some kind or from another traveller on the journey of self-development. In fact, once we start using the Qabalah practically, it is quite amazing how even chance remarks made by other people can offer us meaningful and timely insights into our own nature. Secondly, there is the 'written' Qabalah which traditionally aims to describe the structure and nature of the universe. Thirdly, there is the 'literal' Qabalah which is concerned with the decoding of information within Qabalistic texts, particularly the Bible. In later chapters of this book, we will see how, from a Qabalistic viewpoint, the Bible reads very differently from the orthodox Jewish or Christian viewpoints.

The fourth division is called the 'symbolic' Qabalah and is concerned with the understanding and integration of our own experiences in life, where everything with which we relate is viewed as a symbolic representation of something deeper. The symbolic Qabalah is primarily based on the Tree of Life diagram. Finally, the fifth division is called the 'practical' Qabalah and is concerned with the utilization of all the various aspects of the Qabalah to promote evolution and to create changes on all levels.

As well as being a system of personal development and self-realization, the Qabalah, more particularly, can be seen as:

- a map of levels of awareness and energy
- a means for the correlation and expression of experience
- a tool for communication,
- a method for the expansion of consciousness
- a way to connect inner and outer awareness
- a method for understanding other peoples' experiences
- a way of formulating ideas with more clarity
- a way of relating to all symbols, whatever their source
- a method for testing the 'truth' of any experience
- a means for communicating with other beings, even those that may seem to inhabit other worlds or planes of existence.

THE TREE OF LIFE

When you first look at the Tree of Life (diagram 1) it appears very complicated, but really it is easy to memorize and visualize. Basically it is composed of three triangles, with a circle or sphere (called a Sephirah) at each angle.

The top triangle represents the Spirit that is within us and at the same time universal, common to everyone and everything else. The middle triangle represents the soul, the individual spark of the universal Spirit that has, as it were, broken off to form the core of each living being. The bottom triangle represents the personality; the body, feelings and thoughts with which the soul has 'clothed' itself so that it may come into manifestation. The Tree of Life, therefore, is a complete map of consciousness. It is relevant to everything from the whole universe to each individual being. It represents, through its three basic triangles, the evolution of the individual, and through this, the evolution of the whole universe. Through recognizing and owning everything that we are, we not only

3

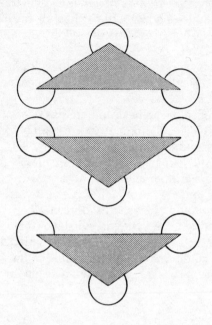

Diagram 2   The Three Triangles

develop ourselves but we come to a greater understanding of the workings of our universe.

Being easy both to visualize and memorize, the Tree of Life serves as a useful and potent guide to the individual human being. It helps you to be exactly who you are right at this moment, and to understand more fully where you have come from and where you wish to go to. It is useful to look at where you have come from and to understand the experiences you have had so that you can learn from them. It is useful to know exactly where you are, which is always here and now. It is also helpful to feel a link with the future, not in the sense of a fortune teller with a crystal ball telling you that you are going to meet a tall dark stranger, but so that you can know in what direction you are heading and what are the most appropriate steps for you to take to move in that direction. When you fully comprehend the guidebook called the Qabalah you tune into the past, the present and the future, bringing harmony to your heart, health – in the sense of wholeness – to your whole being, and connection to everyone and everything else.

The Tree of Life is composed of eleven spheres, the nine which are at the points of the three triangles, and two further spheres positioned thus:

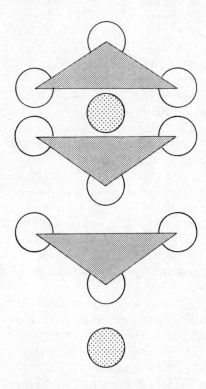

Diagram 3   The Eleven Spheres

The sphere at the bottom of the Tree, from where we always start Qabalistic explorations, is called Malkuth. Representing our senses, and the planet Earth itself, it is the interface between our inner experience and what happens outside of us. Malkuth, literally 'the kingdom', is also sometimes called 'the gate'. Our senses are just that, the 'gate' through which we experience our world. If I look, for instance, at a painting and start interpreting it, I am looking at it in my own particular way and applying past knowledge and experience to it. I will have thoughts and feelings about what the picture depicts. None of this is Malkuth, which is the direct experience of sensing (in this case, seeing) without putting any interpretation or meaning into it. We will explore this further in the exercise at the end of this chapter. Part of the value of the Qabalah is that it allows us to analyse our personality functions and understand how each works separately. We can then 'reconstruct' ourselves in a new way that includes more of ourselves and which makes us feel more whole.

All the spheres on the Tree of Life have innumerable correspondences. Malkuth, for example, as well as corresponding to the Earth and our senses, has animals, plants, minerals, gods and goddesses, trees, elements, letters and numbers attributed to it. As this sphere is about our primary experience, what we sense when we are 'grounded' in our bodies, its correspondences will appropriately match this attribution. The animals associated with Malkuth include the dog and the bull as very earthy creatures. You might like to think what other animals you would attribute to the element of earth. The oak would be an obvious tree to attribute here, for it represents strength and closeness to the planet in a way no other tree does.

Many correspondences will vary, of course, according to our personal connections and our cultural background, although some correspondences do have a more universal nature.

At the top of the Tree of Life is the sphere called Kether, which represents the most central, or deepest, aspect of our Spiritual being, the place where our individuality blurs into union with all other consciousness. The spheres between Kether and Malkuth, and the complex array of paths that connect them, represent all the other aspects of our being. All the spheres have correspondences like those mentioned above which we can directly experience, therefore adding to our knowledge of the different parts of ourselves.

USING THE QABALAH

The Tree of Life helps us to clarify our inner experiences. When we have a clearer idea of what is inside us, of who we are, then we can more easily find ways of expressing ourselves. This is particularly important for our interpersonal relationships, because through the correspondences of the Tree we can relate to the experience of other people, however apparently diverse they appear to be. For example, your god and mine might not have the same name, but once we understand the correspondence and essential identity between the two, we are on a path towards mutual understanding.

The Qabalah helps us to understand symbols, whether experienced in myths, fantasies or dreams. If I have a nightmare, for instance, that involves being chased by a black dog down a dark tunnel, at the end of which is a light I never can quite reach, I might understand this as representing a journey into my unconscious. The light at the end of the tunnel may be a glimpse of the sphere at the centre of the Tree, which is associated with inner harmony; I could then use the Tree to help me reach that light. This might be accomplished through any of a variety of techniques for this purpose: continuing the dream in a conscious visualization, meditating on the corresponding symbols for that sphere, or simply through the increased awareness such a connection inevitably brings.

The spheres on the Tree of Life also correspond to the human body. Using the Qabalah, we can come to a greater understanding of our body energies and the relationship within us between physical, emotional and mental energies. This has great importance therapeutically, and many people who work with others as helpers, whether as direct body workers, counsellors or psychotherapists, find the Qabalistic map most useful. For example, I might see the tension in my solar plexus as an expression of the relationship between the two spheres which correspond to that area of my body. These spheres also correspond to the thinking and feeling functions. By bringing about a stronger relationship between these two functions, perhaps by allowing my feelings more expression and not worrying about what I think I should do, I harmonize

7

these spheres on the Tree and the original tension is lessened.

The sphere which is at the centre of the Tree of Life is called Tiphareth and represents in the solar system the sun and in the human system the heart. Both the sun and the heart are at the centre, so Tiphareth also represents the centre of our psychological make-up, our own individual 'I', self or core identity. Whatever we may know about the solar system, and the fact that the earth goes round the sun and not vice versa, along with all our ancestors we experience the sun as being 'born' each morning, going through the day, then sinking and 'dying' at night, to be reborn again the next day. Our experience of human life is the same: we are born, we live and then we die and, if we believe this, we may be reborn again sometime in the future.

If we can step from our terrestrial consciousness to a place on the sun, the view we have of the solar system is very different. Now the light is continuous and everything revolves around us at the centre or heart of the system. It is the same with our experience as living beings. We can step to our centre and live from there. Life is then continuous and, from this centre, we can harmoniously direct our lives. This harmony is the pure experience of Tiphareth. We can have ideas, concepts, feelings, emotions and sensations about this experience, but there is something beyond all these – the pure unattached quality of harmony. Using the Tree of Life can help us connect with this harmony.

The ultimate goal of the Qabalah is the full, living realization of this harmonious connection. This not only aids in the development of the individual, but also furthers the cause of international and planetary peace. Given the unquestionable importance of these causes, the Qabalah is perhaps more relevant now than ever before.

Exercise 1: The Realization of Malkuth

To start this exercise simply clap your hands together as hard and as loud as you can until you feel tingling in your palms. Then simply hold your hands in the air and experience the tingling sensation.

Notice what you think about doing this, and any feelings it evokes. Perhaps you feel silly clapping your hands for no reason, perhaps you are wondering where this exercise is leading you. Any thoughts or feelings you are having are not the experience of Malkuth. Malkuth corresponds with the human body and the senses – any sensation, such as the tingling you have just been experiencing in your hands, is an experience of Malkuth. Once you do something with this – think about it, have an emotional reaction to it, anything at all – you are working with other spheres, not Malkuth.

Now clasp your two hands together in whatever way you wish, and notice the sensation of one hand against the other. You may have reactions again, such as perhaps thinking about prayer. Without rejecting these reactions or effects, pay no attention to them; they are not Malkuth. Simply experience the sense of touch, one hand against another. This, alone, is the pure experience of Malkuth.

Now look at any picture or photograph, perhaps a picture or poster on your wall, in a magazine, a newspaper, wherever. Once you start thinking about the subject of the picture, or having an emotional reaction to it, you are no longer experiencing Malkuth. You experience Malkuth by paying attention to what your eyes see and by not paying attention to the subject. It is not easy, but try doing this for a little while.

Finally, speak out loud any words and listen to your voice without interpreting what it is you are saying. The sound of the words, totally devoid of meaning, is an experience of Malkuth. Once we understand the words or react to them, we are no longer just in Malkuth.

There is no implication intended here that there is anything wrong with having thoughts, feelings, memories, emotional reactions and so on, or that you should suppress them in any way. All of these things belong to other spheres on the Tree of Life. The purpose of not paying attention to them is to allow you to experience Malkuth on its own.

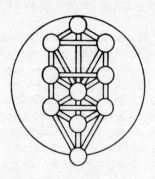

2 · HISTORY AND RELEVANCE

We see in the Tree of Life a glyph of the soul and the universe, and in the legends associated with it the history of the evolution of the soul and the way of initiation.

Dion Fortune

When we look into the history of the Qabalah, we find there are two quite distinct stories. Firstly, there is a 'mythical' history, which, despite its fabulous nature, contains both important 'inner truths' and some incidents based on actual events. Secondly, there is a 'mundane' history which, despite its basis in actual events, also contains fabulous elements. Let's start with the mythical history.

THE MYTHICAL HISTORY

Originally, the Mother-Father of Creation taught the angels a special secret wisdom that forms the basis of what we now call Qabalah. After the creation of humankind and the subsequent fall from grace, the angels decided to teach the Qabalistic secrets to humans to help them regain their link with paradise, paradise being the result of unimpeded manifestation of divine energy on earth. Unfortunately, however, although a few individuals listened to this wisdom and applied it in their lives, the majority of early humans had no time for 'divine plans' and the like, being more interested in mundane affairs.

After many, many generations, the Mother-Father Deity ('God') made a pact or covenant with Abraham, part of which involved the revelation of the Qabalistic wisdom. The central secret was the 'holy name' IHVH (Jehovah) which includes in its four simple letters the key to understanding the entire wisdom of the Qabalah. Abraham transmitted this wisdom to Isaac and Jacob, from whence it was transmitted to Joseph. Unfortunately, Joseph died before telling anyone else the secret, so the knowledge died with him. Abraham had, however, written down some of the more important elements in a book called 'Sepher Yetzirah', which was hidden in a cave.

The Mother-Father Deity decided that it would be appropriate to reveal the wisdom again only when an individual human reached a level of personal and spiritual development where they could ask for it to be revealed. Such a person was Moses. In captivity in Egypt, Moses managed to break the chains of slavery and ignorance through aligning his will and power with that of his highest Self. The Deity recognized his accomplishment and transmitted to him both an exoteric lore (the Ten Commandments) and the secret, inner, esoteric teachings of the Qabalah.

The Deity even gave Moses this new name (we no longer know Moses' original name). The name Moses is composed of the three Hebrew letters Mem, Shin and Heh, representing water, fire and breath. There are many different ways of understanding this name Qabalistically, perhaps the simplest being the most useful – that through conscious breathing techniques we are able to unite the fire and water (or male and female energies) within us. Moses was inspired to write down his understanding in a form that describes the mundane, exoteric teachings but which also describes through allusion, codes and symbolism the secret inner teachings. These writings of Moses compose the first four books of the Bible.

Sometime after Moses, a group of learned and wise holy people came together, in secret, to create a 'mystery college' where the teachings could be taught, understood and, most importantly, practically applied to human affairs, both on an individual and collective level. As well as having a direct oral line of understanding of the Qabalah stemming from the original teachings given to Moses, they also rediscovered the teachings that Abraham had written down and hidden in a cave many centuries earlier. All our current knowledge of the Qabalah stems from this source, and this group of initiates have been known by various names throughout history – the Hidden Masters, Secret Chiefs, Invisible College, and so on.

There are, of course, many differing versions of the mythic history of the Qabalah and this version brings together the elements of several different traditions to create a coherent, if fantastic, tale. Compare it now, if you will, with the more ordinary – and yet no less extraordinary – mundane history of the Qabalah.

THE MUNDANE HISTORY

The two central books of Qabalistic wisdom and understanding are called 'Sepher Yetzirah' (Book of Formation) and 'Zohar' (Book of Splendour). These two books form the basis of all subsequent Qabalistic teaching and development. No one really knows who wrote these books, or if they were originated by the writers or simply the recording of a much older oral tradition.

The Sepher Yetzirah was written before the sixth century AD, possibly by Rabbi Akiba, an enlightened Jewish mystic, around AD 100. It is composed of less than two thousand words. Despite this brevity, however, it concerns itself with the origins of the universe and the central importance of humanity within the universe. It stresses the importance of the Hebrew Alphabet as a key to understanding the universe. The Sepher Yetzirah is, at least potentially, so erudite and wise that many scholars believe that Akiba was definitely recording the findings of an ancient tradition rather than just his own revelations.

The Zohar was possibly written by Rabbi Simon ben Jochai, a contemporary disciple of Akiba. Akiba was executed by the

Romans and Rabbi Simon fled to the hills, hid in a cave, and wrote the Zohar, basing his teachings on the wisdom of Moses. A central theme in the Zohar is that everything in the universe is connected to everything else and that every part of creation is in constant interaction and interplay with every other part. Underlying this 'cosmic dance' there is a hidden order and meaning. This hidden meaning can best be discovered through direct engagement with the things of the earth rather than through attempts to transcend the world.

Both the Zohar and the Sepher Yetzirah stress the importance of a female counterpart to 'God', thus the term I used earlier, the 'Mother-Father Deity'. The Zohar contains imagery of an erotic nature, and a direct link is made between sexual and spiritual union. Indeed, it is through the uniting of the male and female within ourselves that we can truly mirror the cosmic Deity which is a complete synthesis of masculine and feminine energies.

Little more is heard of the Qabalah until a new explosion of interest in thirteenth-century Spain. One of the most influential early books in this period was called 'Sepher Bahir' (Book of Brilliance) which postulated a vast, unseen, multi-layered cosmic reality beneath our more usual, everyday waking 'reality'. Then, in the early fourteenth century in Spain, a Rabbi called Moses de Leon published a version of the Zohar and these mysteries became available to many more mystics and scholars alike. Some people have suggested that Moses de Leon actually invented the Zohar, but even if that were true it would not change the great influence it had on the development of Jewish mysticism and subsequently the Western Mystery Tradition.

There was at that time enough of the teachings available for individuals to start applying them in the intended practical way. One of the greatest of these inner pioneers was born in Spain at the end of the thirteenth century. Abraham Abulafia had little or no formal training but at the age of thirty-one he gained spiritual enlightenment through Qabalistic practices which involved the use of special body postures and breathing techniques. Abulafia became a well-known figure in his time and was disliked by both the Jewish and non-Jewish orthodoxy for his ability to use his clear insights and personal experience to cut through intellectual arguments and outmoded ritual. At one stage he was arrested and was to be burned by the papal authorities, only to be 'saved' when the Pope died during the night before the intended execution. For some reason they set Abulafia free after this, perhaps because they feared others might meet a similar fate as the Pope if they attempted to silence him!

During the middle ages, the Qabalah flourished throughout Europe but particularly in the Hebrew community of Safed in the Holy Land. By the end of the sixteenth century two 'schools' of Qabalistic thought had established themselves, that of Moses Cordovero and that of Issac Luria (who was also known as the 'Ari' which means 'lion'). The Qabalistic teachings were seen as dangerous by orthodox Jewish authorities and were put out of bounds except as an intellectual study for more learned Rabbis. The tradition continued to flourish underground, however.

The next great stage in Qabalistic development happened in the middle of the eighteenth century. A great teacher, Israel ben Eliezer, arose, and became known as the Baal Shem Tov (which means 'bearer of the good name'). The Besht (as he was familiarly known) is the founder of Hasidism (meaning 'devout ones' in Hebrew). The Besht was strongly influenced and affected by Qabalistic theory and practice and by the age of thirty-six showed deep spiritual mastery. He was a very charismatic individual who displayed great spiritual understanding, which he made available to ordinary people. He spoke of his teachings as a 'way of the heart' and stressed that as we are living in this world it is as important for us to enjoy the pleasures of our physical world as it is to pray and practise esoteric techniques.

Despite the fact that Hasidism flourished and is still very alive today, in the changing world of the eighteenth century, Jewish people, like many other people in the Western world at the time of the development of modern mechanistic and economic theories, lost interest in the more practical aspects of their spiritual roots. The orthodoxy prevailed, and it is not until very recent times, and after much Qabalistic development in the Western Mystery Tradition, that there is renewed interest amongst Jewish people in the Jewish Qabalah.

The Mythical versus the Mundane

Perhaps the two histories of the Qabalah are not really so distinct from each other as it appears when they are described in this way. Perhaps both are true in their own ways and whilst the mundane history shows the 'outer' development of Qabalah, the mythical, esoteric history has been running in parallel. Whatever is the truth of this, however, the most important thing is how relevant the Qabalah is to us in the modern world. From my experience, both working on myself and with many other individuals and groups, I know the Qabalah works extremely well as a way of personal, interpersonal and spiritual development. I believe this is what counts to us today, so although the history is of interest, whatever we choose to believe we can experience the direct truth of the Qabalah in our own lives. Much of this work is possible through non-Jewish developments of the Qabalah within the last 150 years or so.

Recent Developments

During the middle to latter half of the nineteenth century, there was an explosion of interest in what we now call The Western Mystery Tradition. Eliphas Levi in France was one of the most influential figures, as were Wynn Westcott and MacGregor Mathers, both founders of the Golden Dawn Mystery School in England. The Qabalah was central to this revival of interest in the esoteric and occult, being the most comprehensive and practical map of human consciousness. All other esoteric lore, inner teachings, mystical approaches, occult practices and so on could be related to the Qabalah and brought into a coherent whole. A system of personal and spiritual growth was developed which could be applied without reference to the Qabalah and yet which was rooted in the theories and practices of the Qabalah.

The interest in esoteric mysteries has continued throughout the twentieth century, with many offshoots of the Golden Dawn and other 'secret societies' flourishing. Certain individuals have also been instrumental in popularizing the Qabalah and its wisdom, notably Israel Regardie, Dion Fortune and Aleister Crowley (who, whatever else may be said about him, was a first-class Qabalist). Rabbi Abraham Isaac Kook, who was chief Rabbi during the founding of modern Israel, expressed interest in Jewish mysticism and the Qabalah and, particularly since the beginning of the 1960s, there has been a renewed interest in Jewish spiritual traditions. The name of Gershom Scholem immediately springs to mind as someone helping to establish a practical, modern-day, working version of Jewish Qabalah.

It has been suggested that the different Qabalistic threads can be given different transliterations of the Hebrew word QBLH to help distinguish them. Thus 'Qabalah' refers to the Western Mystery Tradition version, 'Kabbalah' to the Jewish and 'Cabala' to the Christian version. Whilst there is some value in such a distinction, particularly as the aims and methods of different schools of Qabalah can vary considerably, this idea falls down on two main points. Firstly, writers and workers in the different schools often continue to use the three versions of QBLH without this distinction being made, and secondly – and more importantly – what really matters is the work done, not what it is called. Qabalah, Qabbala, Kabbalah, Kablah, Cabala . . . these are labels, and when we wish to tune into our own inner wisdom, what matters is whether the system works for us.

THE WESTERN MYSTERY TRADITION

The Western Mystery Tradition includes all the esoteric knowledge and teachings that come from 'the West' rather than those originating in 'the East' such as Yoga and Tantra. The disciplines of the Western Mystery Tradition include, therefore, Alchemy, Gnosticism, faery traditions, runes, tarot, various other occult sciences and arts, and the Qabalah. Indeed, the Qabalah has been described as the foundation of the Western Mystery Tradition, and it is true that it underpins much modern theory and practice. Some strands of the Tradition are undoubtedly quite distinct and in no way originate from the Qabalah. One of the particularly useful – I would even say wonderful – aspects of the Qabalah, however, is its ability to include everything else through the system of correspondences. Not only differing aspects of the Western Mystery Tradition, but also all other systems of personal and spiritual development, whatever their origin, can be related back to the Tree of Life. This includes all the Eastern traditions.

It is possible to describe the central, cohesive structure of any esoteric system as its 'Qabalah', so sometimes we hear people talk of 'the Greek Qabalah', 'the Chinese Qabalah', 'the English Qabalah' and so on. Sometimes such descriptions are based on a system of numerology where each letter of the language involved is given a numerical equivalent. Once this is achieved all the other correspondences will fit into the scheme. In the more strict sense, it is certainly dubious and even verging on the absurd to refer to a 'Chinese Qabalah' or 'English Qabalah'. On the other hand, if these systems work in a practical and meaningful way for those applying them to their own growth and initiation, all well and good. And as these systems will inevitably correspond with the Qabalah of the Western Mystery Tradition to which we refer here, they are perhaps not as outlandish as may at first appear. After all, if the aim of greater wisdom and understanding is achieved, does it really matter if the method is idiosyncratic?

Furthermore, if these other 'Qabalahs' lead to delusion and glamour, perhaps this is chiefly due to the practitioners rather than their system – after all, our Qabalah can also be misused by those who wish to bolster their own egos or acquire power over others. Working within a tradition does offer some level of safeguard against these pitfalls, for to progress fully with Qabalistic initiation involves a transcendence of temporal ego and a surrender to the deeper forces within. Such a surrender almost automatically precludes the possibility of using the system for selfish gain.

RELEVANCE TO THE MODERN WORLD

The Qabalah is relevant to our modern world in that it fosters personal, interpersonal and spiritual development. It can be used for any or all of these purposes, either singly or in combination. In fact, what we find is that when we start developing ourselves individually, interpersonal and spiritual repercussions inevitably follow; if we start on a path of spiritual development it affects our personal and interpersonal life, and so on. One cannot be truly separated from the other. We are not individual personalities who somehow 'have' or 'don't have' a soul, a Spirit, relationships with other people. The practical everyday reality of our lives, once we become aware of ourselves in this way, is that we are an interconnected web of different aspects with a 'centre' or 'soul'. It is nearer the truth, therefore, to say that we are individual souls, connected through a common, universal Spirit. Each soul has a personality composed of thoughts, feelings and sensations to experience the world and express itself. This is the vision of the Qabalah, the three parts – Spirit, soul and personality – clearly defined in the three triangles of the Tree.

In terms of individual development and growth, the Qabalah can be seen as a 'guidebook' to what is happening to us at each and every moment. We can use this guidebook to help us define where we are with reference both to where we have come from and where we wish to go. From this perspective we can then work on developing all parts of our being – our physical being, including our body and our senses, our mental being, including both our more abstract and our concrete thinking processes, and our emotional being, including our feelings, values and our emotional reactions. We will see this possibility applied in various ways throughout this book.

By using the Tree of Life as a guidebook to ourselves, we can clarify what 'makes us what we are'. When we analyse ourselves in this way, it is then possible to begin a process of conscious synthesis, putting our different aspects together in a more coherent, holistic way. An analogy has been made between the Tree of Life and a filing cabinet (or a computer database). Every new experience or piece of information that we receive can be related to our existing body of knowledge and understanding. For example, if I am studying a book about philosophy, I can be pretty sure that most of the insights therein correspond to the sphere called 'Hod' on the Tree, for this is the sphere of mind and intellect. Or if I am working on clearing and changing some of the past events in my life which have restricted my free expression, I will probably be working with the sphere called 'Yesod', which has to do with the depths of the unconscious.

When we can relate to information and experience in this way, it helps our interpersonal life, for it allows us to relate to the experiences of other people, however apparently diverse. You may worship the god 'Thoth' and I may worship 'Hermes' – through the Qabalah we will find a strong identity between these two deities. Your god may not be the same as my god, but if we discover their essential similarities, we no longer need to argue about who is 'right' or 'wrong'. The Qabalah allows us to have a living meaningful understanding of symbols, myths and dreams, not based on some fixed or finished description of what symbols may mean, but through the relationship between any symbol and the direct, living experience of the person seeing the symbol.

The Qabalah is very useful to people who work with others in a therapeutic way, whether as psychotherapists, counsellors, healers, or in body therapies. Through its methods and practices, we can learn to understand the relationship between different energies. We are then in a position to foster what is sometimes called 'balance through inclusion'. This means, for instance, if someone has highly developed mental energies and much less developed emotional energies, we will create a balance through encouraging and 'elevating' the emotional energy until it reaches the same level as the mental energy. What we would not do is to bring the mental energy down to the level of the emotional. Through heightening the energy which is less developed, we grow through inclusion, always becoming more rather than less.

The Qabalah can also be applied to more direct spiritual development, whether it has a 'mystical' or 'magical' flavour. A 'mystic' sees the world, is unhappy with it in some way or another, so follows practices that attempt to 'rise above' or transcend the world. 'I don't like it here so I'll go somewhere else', is the catchphrase of the mystic. The magician, on the other hand, feels the same discontent with the world but rather than transcending it, attempts to bring more 'spiritual' energy into manifestation. 'I don't like it here so I'll do all I can to change it', is the catchphrase of the magician. Whether our inclination is to the mystical or magical path, we can use Qabalah for both.

As we have already learned in Chapter 1, the sphere at the bottom of the Tree of Life (Malkuth) is related both to the body and the external physical world. This is most appropriate when we consider that in all Qabalistic work we stress the importance of bringing our work back to ground. There is no point having great insights, making spiritual connections, balancing our inner energies or whatever, if this remains an abstract idea rather than a living reality. If we connect with harmony through our Qabalistic work, for instance, the most important question would be: how can we express this harmony in our everyday life? It may only be a little thing – giving someone we know a hug for example – but each time we ground or earth our experiences we make them real. The Qabalah has been described as 'a living temple of the spirit' – it is only a *living* temple when the spirit is brought alive through its use. This is always our ultimate aim.

QABALAH AND MODERN SCIENCE

In this century, modern science, particularly physics, has moved away from the older mechanistic approach and now conceives the world in a more holistic fashion. It is believed, for instance, that even in the realm of sub-atomic particles which can only be measured through complex and sophisticated equipment, the role of the experimenter plays a vital part. What the experimenter believes actually changes the results of the experiment! Everything (yes, literally everything!) is interconnected, all part of one organic unity. This is, of course, the view shared by many mystics of all persuasions through the ages, and the Qabalah is no different. The work of modern science makes discoveries and pronouncements that echo the words of spiritual masters. The so-called 'objectivity' of the scientific method is seen for what it is – useful for experimentation that is definable within those terms, but unreal for work that explores the meaning and structure of our universe where all matter is alive with energy and potential.

We affect our universe: do not miss the importance of these simple words – we affect our universe. It is important that we bring more consciousness into our actions, for if we affect our world then we are each responsible for the part we play. If I squirt an aerosol can that harms the atmosphere I can no longer say: oh well, what difference does my one little act make? Every act we perform does make a difference. Similarly with our inner work, every act has an effect. This is the central message both of holistic sciences and of the Qabalah.

Exercise 2: The Qabalistic Diary

Before starting this exercise, make yourself comfortable, close your eyes and take a few deep breaths. Be aware that you are a unique individual, choosing, at this very time, in this very space, to utilize your energies to enter into realms of magickal consciousness.

Imagine you are standing in a field at the bottom of a hill. Look around you. Be aware of everything you can see. Take some time to build a clear picture of this field and your surroundings. Utilize your other senses: What can you smell? What can you hear? Perhaps the grass is long, maybe there are flowers blooming in your meadow. Perhaps you can see the sun shining on early morning dew. Let an image of this meadow clearly form around you.

Walk across the field to a path which slopes upwards towards a hill. Take your time to really feel your feet on the ground as you walk across the field. Be aware of what is around you. . . .

Start walking along the path that gently slopes up the hill. Notice the terrain – what plants are there? How does the air smell? Take your time and enjoy your walk. . . .

When you are about half way up the slope, stop for a rest. Look back on the path you have travelled, and down to the fields below. Breathe in the air and feel refreshed and strong. Enjoy the sense of being alone in the beauty of nature. . . .

Just as you are about to continue your journey, you notice something faintly glistening under a nearby rock. You go to investigate and, digging some earth and stones out from around it, you discover something wrapped in a golden cloth. Brush the dirt and dust off the wrapping, unfold it and see before you a book with a beautiful cover. Lift it up to the light. You feel excited and alive as you do this. This book is filled with energy. What colour is it? What shape is it? What designs may there be on the front? Let the image of this magickal book become clear in your imagination.

Apprehensively you open the book and discover that the pages are pure white and completely blank. You now fully realize that this is a book for you in which you can keep a record of your Qabalistic adventures and discoveries. You feel thrilled to be in possession of this, your 'magickal' diary.

When you feel ready, start walking to the top of the hill, carrying your new-found book with you. At the top you find a standing stone, about waist high. Place your book on top of this stone. Be aware that the energy of the sun, shining on your diary, charges it and lightens it. Be aware that the energy of the earth, coming up through the stone, also charges and energizes your diary. Allow your book to change size, colour or shape, to acquire new designs, or simply become radiant as it receives all this positive energy.

Pick your diary up and hold it in front of your heart. Affirm that in this book you will keep an honest record of your magickal work. Let the energy of the book penetrate through your heart to the deepest, most secret depths of your being. Realize also that the energy from the secret depths of your being can also fill up the book with your own unique truth.

When you are ready, thank the sun and the stone, then walk briskly back down to the field where you started, bringing your Qabalistic diary with you.

Back in the meadow, pay attention to feeling your feet on the solid ground. Open your eyes, bringing your imagined –

and yet soon to be physically real! – diary into your everyday reality.

When we do any Qabalistic or other magickal work, it is important that we keep a record of our journeying, our discoveries and insights, whether they are painful or joyous ones. This record can then help us to attune ourselves to our life journey, affirm our commitment and strengthen our sense of purpose. With such a diary our knowledge can become more accessible to us and our understanding will increase. It is up to you to manifest this so far only imaginary diary into Malkuth. How can you do this?

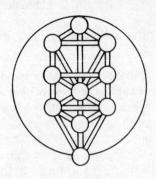

3 · SPHERES AND PATHS

The Qabalah provides a detailed, massive, and coherent world view of the nature of human existence and our relation to the cosmos. Its powerful, poetic vistas have excited the imagination of Jews and non-Jews alike in nearly every country of the globe.
Edward Hoffman

In Chapter 1 we saw how the Tree of Life, although it may look very complicated at first sight, is actually quite simple. It is composed of three triangles, one upright at the top and two upside down triangles beneath. There are nine spheres, one at each of the three points of the three triangles, plus two extra spheres, one between the top two triangles and one at the bottom. (If you need to, refer back now to diagrams 2 and 3 to refresh your memory about this.) In total, therefore, we have eleven spheres on the Tree of Life. The Hebrew word for these spheres is Sephira (plural Sephiroth), which means 'number', and each of the spheres is given a number as shown in diagram 4. Note how the sphere between the two top triangles is not given a number, it is sometimes referred to as 'the sphere without a number'.

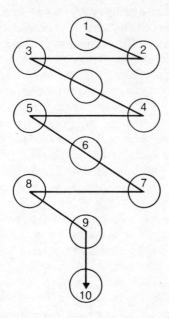

Diagram 4   The Lightning Flash

The other ten spheres are numbered in the order shown by the lightning flash (see diagram 4 again). This is said to be the order of creation – from number 1 (named Kether), which represents the highest or ultimate creator of the universe (and also the deepest, spiritual aspect of ourselves, The Self), to number 10, the sphere named Malkuth with which you connected in Exercise 1. You have already learnt that Malkuth represents the body and senses. It also represents the final result of the creation, the whole physical, manifest world and everything in it.

As well as Hebrew names and numbers, each sphere on the Tree has numerous other correspondences associated with it, ranging from colours, symbols and images through to various gods, goddesses, tarot cards, animals, plants, minerals and so on. In fact, everything that exists (either in reality or in imagination) can be related to the Tree of Life. Some of the main correspondences are shown in diagrams 1 and 5. Each of the spheres also has a primary correspondence which relates it to different aspects of an individual person, and this is shown in diagram 6. Spend a little time now looking at these diagrams of the Tree of Life.

The ten spheres (excluding the eleventh one, Daath) are connected to one another by a complex array of twenty-two paths (see diagram 5). These paths represent the subjective understanding and relationship possible when two particular spheres are connected. For instance, as Hod corresponds with thoughts and Netzach with feelings, the path that connects them represents the relationship between thoughts and feelings. In other words, if you *feel* as though you want to do something but you don't *think* it's a good idea, you are experiencing this particular path. Similarly, if you want to create a connection between your thinking and feeling functions, the correspondences associated with this particular path might help you to make such a link. We will look into these possibilities later in this book.

If we recall the three triangles from which the Tree is basically composed, and compare this with the information in diagram 6, we can see that the top triangle refers to the spiritual aspect of a person, that part of them which is connected to everyone and everything else. This is sometimes referred to as the Supernal Triangle, and is the realm of the *transpersonal*. The middle triangle refers to the individual soul, that part of the total Spirit that has separated, as it were, into an individual spark of soul. The lower triangle refers to the personality, composed of thoughts, feelings, sensations and the subconscious realm.

There are numerous other ways of viewing the Tree of Life through its physical structure. Perhaps the most common division of the Tree is into three pillars. If you look at diagram 1, you can see there is a 'left hand pillar' (with Binah at the top), a 'right hand pillar' (with Chockmah at the top) and a pillar between which is called 'the middle pillar'. These three pillars correspond to the three energy channels said in eastern mysticism to run through the body – the middle pillar relating to the spinal column. When we look at the Tree, we have to remember it is drawn as if we are looking at it overlaying an

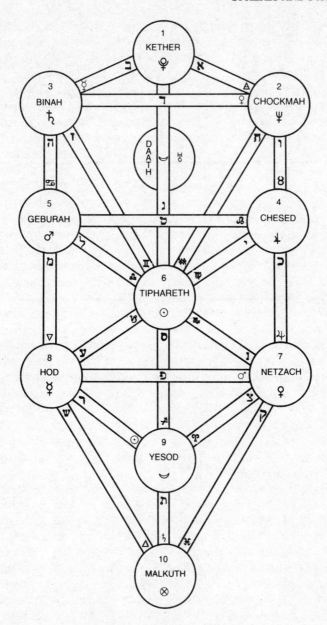

Diagram 5   Correspondences

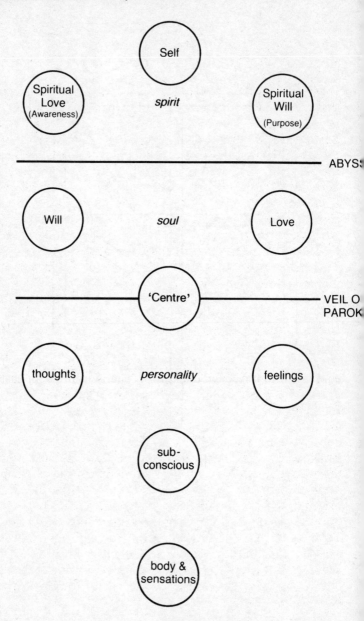

Diagram 6   The Whole Person

individual person. Thus in order to relate it to our own bodies, we have to imagine we turn around and back onto it. In other words, the left hand pillar corresponds to the right of your body, the right hand pillar to the left.

Just because there are 'left hand' and 'right hand' pillars on the Tree of Life, it does not mean that the Qabalistic system is in any way based on a patriarchal, polarized view of life. Some Qabalistic writers have insisted on referring to the two pillars as 'male' and 'female', a dichotomy that is not part of the original map. Of course duality exists, but 'maleness' and 'femaleness' exist on both sides of the Tree. The Tree of Life is based on triangles. To see Hod and Netzach, for instance, as somehow opposed is incorrect. They form a continuum which can only be truly realized and integrated when we introduce a third factor (or position) – in this case either Tiphareth or Yesod. To see Hod and Netzach as somehow 'male' and 'female' is an even greater error – they are both 'male', 'female' and 'neither male nor female'. All Qabalistic writings that suggest otherwise are predicated on a patriarchal world-view that is at the very least outmoded and often directly harmful to the evolution of consciousness.

The Tree of Life has seven planes which are roughly equivalent to the seven chakras or 'energy centres' of eastern mysticism (see diagram 7). If we look at the Tree of Life in detail we can see that, as well as the three triangles already discussed, there are very many more triangles. It is an interesting exercise to see just how many triangles you can spot on the Tree. The whole system is built upon a belief that everything manifests through trinities. When we start studying the physical structure of the Tree of Life, we also find hexagrams (six-pointed stars) and pentagrams (five-pointed stars), circles, crosses and other interesting shapes. The map has been developed over many centuries and it is no accident that all these shapes are included. Even if it was an accident, however, it would not change the value of the map, but would simply increase our wonder at its completeness and effectiveness as a map of consciousness.

It is important to remember that the map is not the territory. This may seem very obvious, but often when we start using

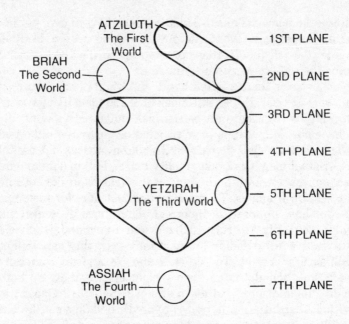

Diagram 7   The Four Worlds and Seven Planes

maps of consciousness such as the Tree of Life we start confusing what the map shows us with our actual experience. Of primary importance is the experience – so the method with the Tree (and any other map of consciousness) is to fit the map to your experience, not try and force your experience into the map. If you do the former, then the map can act as a guide to the territory of life, help you understand your consciousness and grow in the ways appropriate to your individual journey through life.

DEVELOPMENT OF THE SPHERES

To understand the whole Tree, composed as it is of eleven spheres and twenty-two connecting paths, we have to analyse the various aspects in detail. We will start with the spheres, because once we grasp the essential meaning of these, an understanding of the paths comes quite easily. It is important to remember, however, that when we analyse our consciousness in this way, it is essentially an artificial process. In reality, all the different aspects of us are part of one interconnected web of awareness. Our consciousness is then like a spider that moves around on this web, one minute in feelings, the next thinking about something, then lost in memories of the past, planning for the future, and so on.

The value of analysing our functions is twofold. Firstly, and most simply, it helps us to understand ourselves. Secondly, and perhaps more importantly, through analysing ourselves in this way, we move closer to the possibility of creating a harmonious synthesis of our various functions. When such a synthesis takes place, we become able to direct our lives with more clarity, and fulfil our creative and spiritual purpose. As you read the following sections, look at the diagrams in this book to help you understand the description of the spheres.

THE REALM OF THE PERSONALITY

Malkuth – body and senses
Yesod – subconscious
Hod – thoughts
Netzach – feelings

Issues:
Malkuth – increasing sensory awareness and connection, and realizing the importance of the body and physical manifestation.
Yesod – clearing out 'repressed' energies and the subsequent integration of these released energies into their correct sphere.
Hod and Netzach – the balancing of thoughts and feelings, usually achieved through allowing the experience and expression of both.

It is through Malkuth that you have your primary experience of the world. At any moment when you are aware of your environment, you are either seeing, hearing, smelling, tasting, touching or a combination of these. Life is not that simple, however, for when we use our senses to experience the world, or to express ourselves, we inevitably have thoughts and feelings about what is happening. Thoughts are attributed

31

to Hod and feelings to Netzach. If we consider these three spheres on their own, we can say they are the spheres of the present time – all our 'here and now' awareness, wherever we are and whatever we are doing, is some combination of thinking, feeling and sensing.

All of our thinking, feeling and sensing is further affected and coloured by what has happened to us in the past. For instance, I may have had a friendly pet dog when I was a child, whereas you were frequently chased and bitten by a savage dog that lived next door. Now when we are both confronted by a dog on the street, although it may be exactly the same dog, we will both see it differently, particularly in terms of our feelings about it. I might want to go up to it and stroke it, as I am seeing 'dog' as something kind and affectionate. You, however, might already be running away!

This example with a dog may seem rather trivial but it shows how we are affected by the past. It is as if we carry all our experiences from the past within us, and these experiences affect our current perceptions and awareness. If a woman was beaten by her father, it may well affect how she relates to adult men in later life, perhaps always being on guard for a potential attack. She may then be driven by an unconscious need for protection and be unable to make lasting and meaningful relationships with men. Similarly, if someone was over-mothered, perhaps she in turn unconsciously over-mothers her children. All of these incidents from the past that affect us, whether we are conscious of them or not, are attributed to Yesod on the Tree. Part of our work of growth and development in using the Tree of Life is to delve into our past and start releasing the energies that have been blocked there. We can then start to clarify and integrate our perception in the present moment, whatever we are doing.

The four spheres, Malkuth, Hod, Netzach and Yesod, which are found at the bottom of the Tree, represent our personality. As well as dealing with our 'stuff' from the past, as just described, the other main task of our work in this part of the Tree is to create a dynamic and living balance between our thinking, feeling and sensing functions. We relate to the world through these functions, so the clearer we are in understanding and using them, the more effective we become. Also, the more work we do to balance these spheres, the more able we are to receive energies coming from higher up the Tree (or deeper inside ourselves).

There is no suggestion here that we have to be perfect in some way, or have to clear out all our old unconscious material. A true Qabalist will welcome difficulties and problems, not try to transcend them, or gloss over them, but be willing to step right in and work with them, in so doing creating a reality in which they can be transformed into opportunities for growth and development. The first step in this process is almost always acceptance – when we truly accept what is, then we are in the right place to see what we may need to change.

THE REALM OF THE SOUL

Tiphareth – the centred self, 'the silent witness'
Geburah – the archetype of Will and Power
Chesed – the archetype of Love and Awareness

Issues:
Tiphareth – the building of a strong centre for the integration of our everyday relations with the world; and strengthening the connection to deeper, inner energies which may then manifest in our lives.
Geburah and Chesed – the realization of the central importance of the interplay of these archetypes in the unfolding of soul energy on earth.

The sphere at the centre of the Tree, called Tiphareth, is the link between the lower personality spheres and the higher transpersonal spheres on the Tree. The soul, by analogy, can be said to be a similar link between the Spirit and the personality. Tiphareth is usually described as being the 'centre' or the 'I', the little self (with a small 's') that is our individual spark of the bigger Self (with a capital 'S') at the top of the Tree. From the point of view of the personality, Tiphareth is just this. As the 'I', Tiphareth can be understood to be that part of us which is more than body, feelings, thoughts or any combination of these.

If 'I' say that I have a feeling, I have a thought, I have a sensation, then the 'I' that has these things is Tiphareth. Instead of being a player in the drama of life, I can become the director. This is not to become remote and aloof, but rather to be a director who is willing to play a part, to connect with feelings and thoughts and really engage in the world. Qabalistic work is not only about achieving deeper or higher states of consciousness in which we dis-attach from the mundane; it is equally about bringing this awareness to play in our everyday life.

When we become more centred in ourselves, we become more in control of our own destiny, and our own ability to stay in touch with the unfolding of the soul's individual purpose. We experience this through the archetypes of Love and Will as represented on the Tree by Chesed and Geburah. The interplay between these archetypes sets up issues and events in our lives through which we can realize our own inner divinity. We must not confuse these archetypes with the soul, but rather see them as the vehicles for its manifestation in the same way as the lower spheres on the Tree are seen as the vehicles of the personality.

THE REALM OF THE SPIRIT

Binah – Spiritual Love
Chockmah – Spiritual Purpose
Kether – the Divine Self

Issues:
For these three spheres, our work involves both allowing and experiencing spiritual energies through their direct realization.

The spheres above Geburah and Chesed are divided from the Tree below by the Abyss which represents the gulf between phenomenal reality and true spiritual connection. The spheres above the Abyss represent levels or states of awareness that we may only experience directly during the deepest, most meaningful moments in our life, sometimes called 'peak' experiences, when we feel at one with nature and all of life, when we feel Joy, Truth, Beauty and other Qualities that can be attributed to the Spirit, or the deepest connection within us. Fortunately for us, however, we can also experience these Qualities in our everyday world, for Tiphareth also acts as a channel so these energies 'come through' into our waking, ordinary reality.

Every time it feels good to be alive, every time you stop and hear a bird sing and feel wonder, or watch a child playing and feel moved, every time you experience clarity and insight where you know what is the 'right' thing for you to do, or those times when we become so immersed in movement, dance, or physical activity that we seemingly lose all other awareness and simply tune into the physical world, all these times are direct experiences of the transpersonal realms represented by these spheres. We may not be in some pure, transcendent state where we experience unadulterated peace, for instance, but if we simply stop for a moment and experience peace in an everyday act it is no less real or meaningful. One of the main aims of all Qabalistic work, as stressed throughout this book, is to manifest spiritual reality in the everyday world.

PATHS TO CONNECTION

As already described, many of the spheres are connected to others by paths (see diagram 5). These paths represent the subjective understanding and relationship possible when a connection is made between two particular spheres. As an example, consider Malkuth and Netzach. Malkuth relates to the body and Netzach to the feelings, so the path between them shows the relationship between feelings and body. It is a commonly held psychological belief, born out by the experience of therapists who work directly with body energies, that when we repress different emotions and feelings, aspects of their energy become held or deposited in the muscles and tissues of the body.

From this viewpoint, it is possible to deduce two ways of working to release these withheld feelings. We may find ways to access directly the memories associated with the feelings involved, then allow ourselves to re-experience them. This will then release some of the holding in the physical body. Alternatively, we may work directly on the body to release what is held there, thereby causing a release of the repressed feelings involved. The first way is working with this path from Netzach down through to Malkuth; the second way is working up the path from Malkuth towards Netzach.

Another way of working directly with the connections between the spheres is through what is often called 'path-working'. We will look into this more deeply in Chapter 7. There are many ways of pathworking. One of the commonest is to imagine oneself passing through a door that leads to one of the paths, using the associated symbols, including the Hebrew letters, placed prominently on the door, to guide one into the appropriate imagery. We could plan a journey to Tiphareth, for instance, starting in Malkuth, travelling the path to Hod, experiencing Hod, then travelling the path to Tiphareth from Hod. It is important when doing this work to return back to the ground (Malkuth) after each pathworking, partly so that the energy can be grounded, partly so the practitioner does not become 'spaced out'.

As with the spheres, all the paths have numerous corres-pondences associated with them – images, symbols and ideas of all kinds that help describe the energies involved with that path. One of the most commonly used symbol systems associated with the path is the Tarot cards. Good Tarot cards (see Further Reading) will have the appropriate symbols drawn on them. For instance, amongst many other correspondences, the path between Netzach and Malkuth is associated with the Hebrew letter Qoph (meaning 'back of the head'), the moon, dogs howling at the moon, menstruation, the beetle, Pisces, and the dark night of the soul. Many of these symbols will be found on the Tarot card 'The Moon' which relates to this path. The Tarot cards therefore can be seen – and used – as compendiums of associated symbols for the paths. It is no coincidence that there are twenty-two trumps in the Tarot so they relate to the twenty-two connecting paths on the Tree.

The ten spheres on the Tree of Life (excluding Daath)

are sometimes referred to as the first ten 'paths', then the other twenty-two paths that connect the spheres are called the eleventh to thirty-second paths. As well as being representations of the connections between the spheres, they are also given a special name and correspondence, thus:

path	connecting spheres	meaning
11th	1–2	scintillating path, facing the creator
12th	1–3	transparent path, seeing of visions
13th	1–6	uniting path, realizing spiritual truth
14th	2–3	illuminating path, fundamental holiness
15th	2–6	constituting path, substance of creation
16th	2–4	eternal path, pleasure of paradise
17th	3–6	disposing path, foundation of faith
18th	2–5	influential path, understanding causality
19th	4–5	activating path, the experience of blessings
20th	4–6	intelligent path, knowledge of existence
21st	4–7	conciliatory path, transmitting divine influence
22nd	5–6	faithful path, increasing spiritual virtue
23rd	5–8	stable path, increasing consistency
24th	6–7	imaginative path, renewal and change
25th	6–9	tentative path, the alchemical processes
26th	6–8	renovating path, life force in action
27th	7–8	exciting path, the nature of existence
28th	7–9	admiral path, understanding the depths
29th	7–10	corporeal path, the formation of the body
30th	8–9	collecting path, celestial arts and astrology
31st	8–10	perpetual path, regulating the creation
32nd	9–10	administrative path, directing life energies

It is well worth comparing these brief, suggestive descriptions with the paths and the spheres they connect. They can greatly aid our understanding not only of the Tree of Life map, but also of the connections within ourselves between differing states of consciousness.

A TREE FOR ALL USES

As already mentioned, in Chapter 7 we will look in more detail at 'pathworking' and active ways of using the energies on the Tree. In Chapter 8 we will look at 'ways of stillness', using the Tree to aid our meditation, contemplation and prayer. In Chapter 9 we will look at ways of using the Tree for healing. As the paths are representations of the subjective connections between the states of awareness shown in the Spheres, whenever and however we use the Tree, we inevitably travel the paths. It is wise Qabalistic practice to remember this and to realize that there is nothing static suggested by the Tree, but that it is a diagrammatic representation of a constantly evolving and changing system. It is also worth guarding against the possibility of getting so caught up in travelling the paths that the point of the work is missed. Whenever we travel on the Tree, our goal is increased self-awareness, integration of the differing aspects of ourselves, and the full and clear manifestation of this work in the everyday, physical world. All paths, in true Qabalistic practice, lead back to Malkuth, the world and the physical body.

Different Qabalists, whether from different schools of practice or simply because they are individuals, use the Tree for different purposes. It is possible to work only with the bottom part of the Tree and use it as a guide to personal self-development. It is equally possible to work primarily with the deeper energies represented by the top part of the Tree, as a method towards spiritual enlightenment. Some people use the Tree to guide their rituals, ceremonies and group practices whereas other people avoid groups at all costs. It is truly wonderful that the Tree can be used in so many different ways and be personalized for individual uses. It is important also, however, to honour the tradition of the system that has been built up over many centuries of practice and experience. If you individualize your Tree so much that it no longer relates to other people's Trees, that is fine for you alone, but removes the possibility of relating your work to others. The Tree is designed so that we can relate our experiences. We do not live in isolation (except those of us reading this book who are hermits in inaccessible caves!). We live in a world where we are in constant relationship with all other beings, human and otherwise. Our life is enhanced when we use the Tree to aid rather than hinder this contact and relating.

All the different approaches and ways of working with the

Tree of Life can enrich our lives through clearing out past conditioning, traumas and controls, dynamically balancing growth in the present, and through making a link to each individual's sense of purpose and meaning. The Tree of Life is a complete map of consciousness and it works best when it is used in its entirety. It is also a holistic model, however, and through using any part of it we are inevitably linked to the whole, for each part, each path and each sphere is not only connected into the whole scheme, but each part itself, whilst undeniably only a part, nevertheless includes the whole.

CORRESPONDENCES

If we consider the correspondences to the spheres again, we can see that we have already met many different ones. For example, we have learnt that Hod corresponds to the number eight, the thinking function, and is an aspect of the personality. We can now start connecting it to other 'universal' correspondences, for instance gods and goddesses primarily involved with the mind, thought and communication (for it is through words, which are in a sense spoken thoughts, that we primarily communicate). Such deities include Hermes (Greek), Thoth (Egyptian) and Mercury (Roman). A planet is associated with each sphere, so here we can fairly clearly attribute Mercury, the planet of communication. Spells, words of power and the element of air will correspond because of their association with the mind.

Many other items are traditionally attributed to each sphere, so in the case of Hod we find the colour orange, the vision of splendour, the precious stone opal, the perfume storax, the animal jackal, the herbs fennel and marjoram, the hazel tree and so on. See if you can work out why some of these items should be said to correspond to Hod. In doing this, you will actually be engaging Hod (thoughts) to do it! With all correspondences, the most important thing is to make your own connections. So, for instance, if in your experience the willow tree and a goldfish are more appropriate correspondences than the hazel tree and jackal, then these will be your personal correspondences for working in the sphere of the mind, Hod.

The whole point of using correspondences is to be able to relate your experience into the Tree, then see the relationship of this with the whole Tree. Any correspondence is appropriate so long as it works for you. It is also useful, however, to stretch ourselves to see why certain correspondences have a more 'universal' application to the spheres. The opal is attributed to Hod, for instance, because it has the varied colours that correspond to Mercury, and the jackal because in the ancient world it was considered sacred to Mercury. In our modern world, however, we may not have much contact with jackals, and think that, for instance, a dog is a better correspondence because of its mercurial nature.

In a work of this size we cannot give long detailed tables of correspondences for all the spheres and paths, but you will find such tables in my work *The Living Qabalah* (see Further Reading). The more correspondences we can connect to the Tree of Life, the more alive the system becomes and the more we are able to relate all our experiences in life – whatever they are and however they manifest – to our total body of knowledge and understanding. It is quite amazing how using the Tree in this way appears to increase our ability to integrate the different aspects of our being.

Exercise 3: Spheres of Awareness

For this exercise simply consider the following attributions relating to the ten spheres on the Tree of Life. These attributions represent the energies attainable when we contact the spheres through travelling the appropriate paths. As you meditate upon the spheres and these attributions, study diagrams 1 and 5.

Malkuth	discovering the mysteries of the physical universe; the ability to discriminate; physical healing and overcoming inertia and sloth.
Yesod	discovering the mysteries of the astral levels and lunar energies; to realize the workings of universal energies; to connect with the divine plan.

Hod	discovering the mysteries of information systems and Mercurial energies; truthfulness; greater ability to communicate clearly.
Netzach	discovering the mysteries of loving sexuality and Venusian energies; unselfishness; increasing artistic creativity.
Tiphareth	discovering the mysteries of beauty and harmony and solar energies; centred consciousness; stimulating the energy of soul manifesting in life.
Geburah	discovering the mysteries of power and the use of Martian energies; purposeful change; awakening inner and outer strength.
Chesed	discovering the mysteries of love and the use of Jupiterian energies; peace and love awakened; stimulating the forces of abundance.
Daath	discovering the mysteries of the shadow side of existence; inner depths explored; knowledge of the rainbow bridge.
Binah	discovering the mysteries of silence and secrecy; increasing understanding; realizing that all things are united.
Chockmah	discovering the mysteries of purpose and initiative; increasing wisdom; realizing the universal plan as manifest through the world.
Kether	discovering the mysteries of unity and union; the inner quest; amplification of spiritual energy and the revelation of divine inspiration.

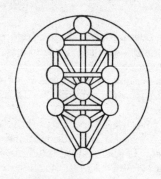

4 · Creation and the Sacred Alphabet

The Qabalah is . . . the repository . . . of the mysteries hidden
since the beginning of time. The diversity is only the expression
of the infinite 'richness' of the one truth and in no way affects
its transcendent and immutable unity.

Leo Schaya

The first sentence of Genesis in the Bible can be transliterated from Hebrew as 'Berashith Bera Elohim Ath Ha Shamaim Va Ath Ha Aretz.' This can be very roughly translated as 'In the beginning God created the heaven and earth.' Once we start looking at these first words of Genesis from a Qabalistic viewpoint, however, we find they contain a lot more than is apparent at first sight. As we learnt in Chapter 2, the words in the first four books of the Bible are attributed to Moses, writing under divine inspiration. It is not surprising, therefore, to find much more hidden within these simple words. There are many different ways to 'read' these words Qabalistically, one version being: 'Out of the universe the light of the sun brought the duality of existence into manifestation, expressing the Spirit through male and female principles. The Mother-Father Deity expressed itself through the cosmic principles represented by the first nine spheres of the Tree of Life and heaven and earth were created.'

If we look at this in more detail we can start to understand how the Qabalah sheds light on our understanding of this creation myth. The first word of the sentence in Hebrew is Berashith, 'In the beginning'. All Hebrew letters have a special meaning attributed to them, and a number. We will look at the numbers in more detail later, but for now let us consider the meaning of the letters in Berashith, or BRAShIT.

Beth = a house or container (the universe);
Resh = the sun;
Aleph = beginning, duality – positive and negative;
Shin = Spirit;
Yod = male principle;
Teth = female principle.

Put this together and we have: 'Out of the universe the light of the sun brought the duality of existence into manifestation, expressing the Spirit through the male and female principles.' Of course, there are many other ways of putting these words together, creating different nuances of meaning. Other possibilities might include, 'the magician with the secret of the universe created the sun in the beginning to bring the Spirit of life through the secret gate of initiation into the manifest universe', or 'the Spirit of god expressed the dual principle of life and death through cosmic manifestation. From this dual principle the first nine spheres of existence were created.' It is not that there is a right or wrong way to understand this word Berashith, more that each individual Qabalist can come to his or her own understanding of the meaning.

If we now consider the word 'Elohim', usually translated as 'God', we find a very interesting mystery. The word ALHIM in Hebrew is composed of a feminine singular ALH with IM, which is a masculine plural, added. The word thus expresses the uniting of male and female principles. This is why I prefer to use the term 'the Mother-Father Deity', for in Chapter 1 of Genesis, when the word 'Elohim' is used, this is closer to what is intended. It is only in Chapter 2 of Genesis, after the creation is fully manifest, that IHVH, Jehovah, is used for 'God'. We will be looking in much more detail at this name of 'God' in the next chapter.

Even the word ATh in Hebrew, composed as it is of two letters Aleph and Teth, and simply translated as 'the', contains a mystery. The letter Aleph is the first Hebrew letter, numbered 1, as is Kether, the first sphere on the Tree of Life. The letter Teth is the ninth Hebrew letter, numbered 9, as is Yesod, the ninth sphere on the Tree. Thus the simple word 'ATh' can be taken to represent the whole Tree minus the final manifestation in Malkuth, when the world itself is formed. This has led some scholars to believe that Genesis refers only to creation in potential. Exodus is concerned with the 'actual' manifestation, after Malkuth is created and when the 'Mother-Father Deity' has formed itself into IHVH, Jehovah, a God with a special message for humankind.

So the creation of the universe as understood Qabalistically is not about a single male God creating everything, but rather a complex unfolding of principles and energies originating from a source that includes both 'male' and 'female' energies. It is worth stressing that this interpretation is not the product of some strange, esoteric fantasy, but is very closely based on the original Hebrew text. Let us read it once more: 'Out of the universe the light of the sun brought the duality of existence into manifestation, expressing the Spirit through male and female principles. The Mother-Father Deity expressed itself through the cosmic principles represented by the first nine spheres of the Tree of Life and heaven and earth were created.'

To a Qabalist, the Mother-Father Deity is seen as pure immanence, present in everything, manifest and unmanifest. When this Deity created the manifest universe that we know, through the words 'let there be light', it was creating a duality – for if there is light then implicitly there is also dark, and it was through this duality that everything else could come into being. The Mother-Father Deity is present in both the light and the dark, in the unmanifest and the manifest, in everything at all times. The creation was an act of love, for the purpose of this original division was so that each part or polarity could realize itself as divine through recombining with the opposite polarity. All opposites are in harmonious balance with each other and whenever they unite they mirror the original creation of the universe.

Everything in the Qabalah is seen, however, in terms of trinities rather than dualities. The Mother-Father Deity is simultaneously Female and Male and the creation is the Child, thus creating a threesome. When Christians talk of the Father, Son and Holy Spirit they are referring to the same trinity, for the Hebrew word for 'holy Spirit' is RUACH, which is a feminine noun. Thus the Trinity is Father, Child and Mother. This is also expressed in the Gnostic Deity name, IAO, where I is the Male principle, O the Female principle and A their offspring. The letters I and O are interestingly suggestive of male and female. In the Qabalah the female principle of the Deity is very important and is also known as Shekhinah, of which we will be learning more in a later chapter. Although the Jewish religion (and its Christian offshoot) may have become patriarchal in its current form, its secret inner teachings, as expressed through the Qabalah, are equally inclusive of both male and female.

THE GARDEN OF EDEN

One of the most fascinating myths in the Bible is that of the Garden of Eden, some wonderful place where, according to ordinary interpretation, something went wrong which led to the banishment of humankind from its splendours. In the patriarchal versions of this myth, the fault is placed at the feet of the woman involved – if only Eve had not eaten of that apple we would somehow all still be in this state of bliss. As you may have already guessed, this is not the Qabalistic view.

Qabalists believe that when the world was originally created, the Tree of Life and all that it represents was itself the Garden of Eden. This initial Tree, therefore, represented by the perfect existence in the Garden, does not include within itself the knowledge of duality.

Everything is at one. The creatures who exist in this garden, represented by Adam and Eve, the son and the daughter, have not awakened to the realization that something else exists beyond their perfect garden. They do not realize their separation and difference from one another. From the beginning, however, there was a a shadow side to this Tree, represented by the Tree of Knowledge of Good and Evil.

One day, through the direct intervention of the Mother-Father Deity, Adam and Eve realized that they were different beings, clothed with a different form, one male, the other female. As soon as they realized this, duality was brought into the garden and the Tree of Knowledge of Good and Evil became part of their reality. Once they had awoken in this way, the Deity placed an Abyss between itself and its creation. This division was formed so that the created beings could experience being separate, existing in duality. In this separate existence they had the chance of re-uniting, of bringing their two 'halves' together into union through an act of love. This way they could again realize their essential unity with the Deity and all of creation, transcending their separate existence in the world of duality. We all still have this opportunity, the chance of experiencing our own inner divinity. We can only bridge this Abyss and realize our true selves through love, for it is for the sake of love that we were divided in the first place.

This version of the 'fall' is very different from that often perpetrated, in which we all somehow carry an 'original sin' through which we are doomed unless saved by divine intervention. Rather than 'original sin', Qabalists believe we have 'original grace' and it is through this grace we can come to know ourselves. We can experience this grace only in love, for it is through love that the Deity created the universe. When we experience true Love we are aligning ourselves with the Deity and realizing our own innate divinity.

CREATING THE TREE OF LIFE

We have looked so far at a Qabalistic theory of the creation of the world. There are other theories in the Qabalah, some similar, some quite different, apart from all the other creation theories in other esoteric systems. One of the most valuable aspects of the Qabalah, however, is that we do not have to 'believe' anything. Indeed, it is always stressed that our experience is of much more importance. Naturally we cannot have an experience of 'the creation' – if we were there we do not remember it! What we can do, however, is relate our experience of the world to the various theories and see what fits for us. Then, whatever theory we hold, it is based on our experience rather than something simply told to us. For me the above theory of creation feels good, but I do not 'believe' it is true. I am simply holding it as my current belief which, if my experience and understanding changes, I am quite happy to change. If this happens, however, I would not have to let go of the Qabalah, for all theories can be related to the Tree of Life, which is what makes it such a wonderfully universal system.

If we now consider the creation or formation of the actual Tree of Life itself, we find there is a description of this which, albeit still a theory, is based on numbers, so is a totally non-sectarian and non-biased approach. In following this description of the creation of the Tree of Life, based on the work of Aleister Crowley, we find we also come to a greater understanding of the actual creation of the universe.

The formation of the Tree of Life proceeds from Kether to Malkuth, following the path of the lightning flash (see diagram 4). Above the Tree there are sometimes drawn three veils which represent the absence of anything concrete. Qabalists say this area above the Tree is veiled because this is as far as human knowledge and understanding can reach. It takes a long time to achieve a full understanding of this side of the veils, so we are advised to concentrate our efforts on understanding the manifest Tree, and not bother ourselves unduly about what may come after. If we achieve a true experience and understanding of Kether we are united with the Mother-Father Deity. This is already an accomplishment so beyond our ordinary consciousness that to worry about what might come next seems rather foolish.

The first step in the formation of the Tree is the creation of Kether. A point appears which has neither parts nor magnitude, only position. It is positive, it exists, yet it is completely undefinable. It is the number 1 which is indivisible, and incapable of multiplication or division by itself. It has a position but no other attributes. This does not mean much unless there is another position with which to compare it. This can only be created through the formation of a second point, which then forms (between the two points) a line. The only way the original 1 of Kether can become more is through duplication of itself (by reflection). The second point, Chockmah, is given the number 2 and corresponds to the will or purpose of the original point to duplicate itself.

All we have so far are two points at an indeterminable distance from each other. In order to discriminate between them there has to be a third point, Binah, the number 3. Three points can create a surface, a triangle. Now we are able to define any of these points in terms of its position relative to the other two. Thus an awareness (spiritual awareness) is born. Love is attributed to this third point, as being the agency of true awareness. We have now created the Supernal Triangle, something that has a purpose and an awareness but is still completely unmanifest. There are three points but there is no idea of where any of them exist. Indeed, they are completely unmanifest. A fourth point (not in the plane of the triangle inscribed by the first three points) must arise, which formulates the idea of matter by creating a three-dimensional solid.

The original point in Kether can now be defined by three other co-ordinates. Something solid can exist, manifestation has taken place. The potential has become actual as from an original nothing something has now emerged. This is Chesed on the Tree of Life. This initial 'matter' is exceedingly tenuous, however, for the only property of any given point is its position relative to the other three points. No change is possible, nothing can happen. A fifth point must be formed, and this is the concept of motion, called Geburah on the Tree. Only with motion (and the subsequent creation, through motion, of time) can events occur. Not only is the concrete idea of a point now possible, but the point can become self-conscious, because it can define itself in terms of time and motion – it has a past, present and future. This is Tiphareth, the number 6, the centre of the system, pure self awareness capable of experience within the space-time continuum formed in Chesed and Geburah.

The remainder of the Tree then represents the vehicles which the self-conscious point in Tiphareth forms for its experience and expression. These are feelings (7, Netzach), thoughts (8, Hod) and sensations (10, Malkuth). These three vehicles carry within them their own knowledge and experience of the past represented by Yesod (9, the subconscious). In Malkuth, therefore, the original point's idea of itself is fulfilled and brought into complete manifestation.

This description of the creation of the Tree of Life is very neat in that it bypasses any need to believe in a particular religious or philosophical idea, being based as it is on pure number. Again, however, I would stress that the Tree of Life can be used as a practical, living map of consciousness, and agreement with this description is totally unnecessary. It cannot be over-emphasized that the Tree is what you make of it. It is initially useful, however, to use existing knowledge to make connections and help you build up the Tree until you have your own vibrantly alive Tree of Life in your consciousness. Then your own correspondences and understanding will blossom and the Tree will serve you in your growth and development.

THE SACRED ALPHABET

All alphabets are sacred to those who use them to communicate with other people. To me the English alphabet is very sacred – without it I could not write this book and share with you my understanding of the Qabalah. Without it I could not tell my loved ones how I feel about them. Beyond this 'mundane sacredness', however, certain alphabets have become known as particularly sacred because in their letters we find secret correspondences and meanings that add much to our understanding of ourselves and our universe. Sanskrit is an example of such a language from the East, Hebrew an example from the West. As we have already seen, to understand creation as described in Genesis we need a knowledge of the inner, 'secret' meaning of the Hebrew alphabet.

Indeed, Qabalists believe that the books of the Old Testament written by Moses are all in code and cannot be interpreted unless this code is cracked.

Each Hebrew letter has a specific meaning and a number attributed to it. Each letter is a symbolic representation of a cosmic principle. The letter Aleph, the first letter of the Hebrew alphabet, is given – not surprisingly – the number 1. It is therefore a representation of the principle of Unity. Its specific meaning is 'ox'. At first sight this may seem peculiar, but the meanings are themselves suggestive rather than direct. Many ancient cultures believed that the universe originated from the belly of a cow or an ox-like creature. For example, in Egyptian mythology the goddess Ta-Urt is represented by a hippopotamus and is the mother of all cycles of creation. She is, incidentally, the originator of the Tarot cards (Ta-Urt=Tarot). So by giving the letter Aleph the meaning of 'ox', the suggestion is of the originator, that place from where all else comes. An ox may also suggest strength and purpose, other attributes relevant to the source of all creation.

It was believed by many ancient philosophers, Plato for instance, that the whole universe is based upon numbers. Modern physicists believe the same thing. A number can then be seen as a symbol that conveys an idea. By linking these numbers with the Hebrew alphabet, we have a compendium of understanding that can allow us to comprehend more clearly the universe and our place within it.

There are twenty-two letters in the Hebrew alphabet and they are related to the twenty-two paths on the Tree of Life. They represent the different states of consciousness that are created when the cosmic principles represented by the spheres are connected through human awareness. The letters then represent the essence or principle behind these connections. Beth, the second letter of the Hebrew alphabet, means 'house', but more than this it represents the archetype of all containers, all 'housings' from obvious physical dwellings through to the boundary of the whole of creation. This is why it is the first letter in the first word, Berashith, in the Bible, meaning, as we have learned, 'in the beginning'.

Three of the Hebrew letters correspond to the elements of

air, water and fire – Aleph, Mem and Shin. They are known as the 'mother letters' and it is said all the other letters originate from them. Similarly, in esoteric teachings, it is said everything originates from various combinations of these three elements, air, water and fire. This includes, of course, the fourth element, the earth. These three letters also correspond to the head (fire), chest (air) and belly (water) of a human being.

From these three mother letters arise seven 'double letters' representing the manifestation of duality. These letters (Beth, Gimel, Daleth, Kaph, Pe, Resh and Tau) also correspond to the seven directions (above, below, east, west, north, south and centre) and they have a relationship with the seven 'planets' of the ancients (mercury, moon, venus, jupiter, mars, sun and saturn). In a human being they relate to the seven openings in the head – the two eyes, two ears, two nostrils and mouth. There are twelve remaining letters (He, Vau, Zain, Cheth, Teth, Yod, Lamed, Nun, Samekh, Ayin, Tzaddi and Qoph) which are called the single or simple letters. They correspond to the twelve signs of the zodiac. In the human being they correspond to sight, hearing, smell, speech, taste, sex, work, movement, anger, humour, imagination and sleep.

As we can now see, the twenty-two letters of the Hebrew alphabet are more than simple representations of sounds. T-H-E in English is simply a representation of the sounds that make up a word for the definite article. In Hebrew the two letters Aleph and Teth (that make up the Hebrew word for 'the', ATh) have correspondences that would lead to a deeper understanding of the word represented by these letters. This was described earlier, Aleph being the first letter and Teth the ninth, thus representing the nine archetypes of all existence that come into manifestation in 10, Malkuth. 10 in Hebrew is the letter Yod which as well as 'hand' also means 'seed', the seed out of which all else grows.

Words of the same numerical value are considered to be explanatory of each other and the art of understanding these relationships is called Gematria. It is the basis of Qabalistic numerology. Appendix 1 shows the Hebrew alphabet with its primary meaning and numerical equivalents. For instance the Hebrew word for love is AHBH. A=1, H=5, B=2 and H=5; so the numerical value of this word is 13. The Hebrew word for Unity is AChD. A=1, Ch=8, D=4, so the numerical value of this word is also 13. Therefore, through Gematria, we can say that Love and Unity are equivalent!

Another Hebrew word for unity is ALP: A=1, L=30, P=80, a total of 111. The word APL also adds to 111 and means darkness, as does the word ASN (A=1, S=60, N=50) which means sudden death. At first sight it may seem difficult to relate unity, sudden death and darkness together, but the key to such understanding can always be found through meditation. There will be various ways of interpreting this relationship. The numerical identity between these three words may mean, for instance, that individual consciousness is annihilated in Unity and at the threshold of Unity there is darkness.

Gematria may seem like nonsense at first sight. If we think of Zen koans they may also initially seem like nonsense: silly stories about the sound of one hand clapping, for example. Their intention, however, is to transcend ordinary reality and create a mystical level of consciousness where insights about oneself and the universe can occur. The same is true of Gematria and the excitement of making a personally meaningful connection between two or more apparently disconnected words or phrases has to be experienced to be understood.

Exercise 4: The Holy Chalice

In Exercise 1 we connected to Malkuth (the senses), using the exercise to differentiate between what we were directly sensing (Malkuth) from what we thought about it (Hod) and what we felt about it (Netzach). When we thought or felt something about what we were experiencing it was said to be 'not Malkuth'. As you may well be aware by now, when you had thoughts and feelings they were experiences of Hod and Netzach and the paths that connect these to Malkuth. In the following exercise you will be choosing to work directly with these two spheres, and then seeing how we can bring all three named spheres together in our work.

Firstly, therefore, I am going to ask you to connect with Hod. To do that, all you have to do is simply think about something because once you are thinking you are using Hod. I am going to ask you to think specifically about the holy grail, a magical cup, or a chalice. If I could supply you with all the materials and skills you would need for this, what kind of chalice would you make? Spend some time now thinking about this – would it be a simple or elaborate cup, would it be made of metal or wood – which type? – would it be simple or encrusted with jewels . . .?

When you have thought about this chalice for a while, it is a good idea if you either draw a representation or write a description of it, to get a clear picture of what your chalice looks like. When you are ready, continue with the exercise.

Sit in a comfortable position, relax and close your eyes. Imagine you are in a wood, surrounded by light, young trees. Smell the fresh air around you, and allow yourself to really 'be' in this place. Feel your feet on the ground, imagine the sun shining through the trees and listen to the bird song or other sounds of which you may be aware. Imagine you have your chalice with you.

As you tune into this place, imagine you can hear a spring bubbling up somewhere nearby and start to walk in that direction. Take your time, noticing what is around you, then come to a clearing or grove in the woods and see the spring. In your own time, walk up to the spring and fill your chalice with some of the crystal-clear, sparkling water that is gushing from it.

Drink from your chalice. How do you feel doing this? What does the water taste like? What effect does drinking this water from your magic cup have on you? How do you feel now you have imbibed it?

When you are ready, come back to your room, open your eyes and stay with how you are feeling. What was this experience like for you?

A chalice, grail or magic cup is a symbol usually associated with Netzach, which also corresponds to feelings and nature generally. In your imaginary journey to the spring you have travelled to this sphere. You started in Hod, thinking about your chalice, then you experienced drinking from this cup, having feelings associated with this, and perhaps some effects on your consciousness. In this exercise you have used both Hod (thoughts) and Netzach (feelings) and made a connection between them. As in all Qabalistic work, it is now important for you to ground this experience in Malkuth, the body and external world. How can you express what you have connected with from this exercise in your everyday life?

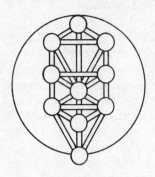

5 · DIFFERENT WORLDS

The essence of the whole is a four letter name ... this name is the key to understanding all that humanity can comprehend concerning the nature of the whole of reality. Look carefully at the name itself. It suggests what God might look like.

Jeff Love

Our physical bodies are not just composed of cells, molecules, tissues, organs, skin, blood and the like. They are also composed of various different kinds of energy. For instance, there is the energy we use to stay alive, transforming our air and food intake into life energy. Then there is all the energy we use to interrelate with the world, whether in our work or play. We even use energy when we are resting and asleep; indeed, our lives are an ever-changing and never-ending interplay of energies.

Qabalists believe, along with most others who investigate human energies, that there is another body, closely associated with and aligned to the physical body, called the etheric body. We normally only see our physical bodies, but if we could see all the energy being generated within us, as a separate entity, then we would be seeing our etheric 'double'. This etheric double corresponds to Malkuth as does the physical body. One simple way of experiencing your etheric double is to move a finger of one hand closer and closer to the finger of your other hand, until they are nearly but not quite touching. You can then sense the etheric double of each.

There are other energy bodies that correspond to the other spheres and planes on the Tree of Life. The energy body associated with the personality spheres on the Tree, and most particularly with Yesod, is the astral body. This too, whilst closely interwoven with the functioning of the personality through the thoughts, feelings and emotions, is clearly a body in its own right. Sometimes a distinction is made between the 'higher' astral (of Hod and Netzach) and the 'lower' (of Yesod) but this distinction is one of quality rather than kind. The astral double is as real as our thoughts and feelings, albeit of a different order.

We can be aware of our astral double by simply allowing ourselves to relax and sink into an awake but disassociated reverie. Whenever we dream or daydream we are using astral energies. It is as if we are 'in another world', seeing what is happening there and having experiences that, on that imaginative level, are very real. We may be able to open our eyes and be back in the physical world at any moment, but that does not make the experience any less 'real'. And the deeper we allow ourselves to sink into the astral world, the more we start experiencing the kind of thinking and feeling associated with these energies.

Our physical, etheric and astral bodies are not really separate, but form a continuum from the physical outwards. They operate at different rates of vibration, but as with the different spheres on the Tree of Life, they are part of one continuous experience (just as the spheres are part of one Tree). This single Tree of Life can be usefully divided into different areas or 'worlds', however, so we can come to a clearer understanding of how our different inner energies function.

THE FOUR WORLDS

If we look again at diagram 7, we see that the Tree of Life can be divided into four 'worlds', or levels of energy. The first world, called Atziluth, is composed of Kether and Chockmah. Kether, in this sense, relates to the Mother-Father Creator and Chockmah to the Creator's will or purpose for coming into manifestation. It is said that the Creator and her/his will are inseparable, so it seems quite natural to include both of these spheres in the first world of energy. It is then referred to as the Creative World, the 'place' from where everything else originates.

The second world, called Briah, is composed of the third sphere alone. It is referred to as the Receptive World. If the Creator has a creative will, then this Creator, to be in balance, must also have a 'receptive' side. In the Qabalistic tradition, all the spheres are both masculine and feminine in their energies so there is no correlation made between 'creative' and 'masculine' and 'receptive' and 'feminine' as in some other systems. Chockmah and Binah, both on the same plane on the Tree of Life, are equal and in dynamic balance with one another. One could not exist without the other.

The result of the interaction between these two worlds is the formation of a third world, Yetzirah, which is composed of all the remaining spheres except Malkuth. This third world is called the Formative World, for it is in this world that all the different aspects that form the final physical manifestation are found. This includes the realm of archetypes (Chesed and Geburah), the soul or individual self (Tiphareth) and the vehicles for manifestation, or 'the personality spheres', represented by Netzach, Hod and Yesod.

The culmination of the process found in these first three worlds is the formation of a fourth, final world, called Assiah, which represents the actual physical manifestation, the world as we know it. For each of us as individual beings, it also represents the body as the physical substance through which we come into being. Sometimes these four worlds are represented by four separate Trees, one for each world, but for all practical intents and purposes it usually makes more sense to stick with the one Tree of Life. As each individual sphere on the Tree is said to have a complete Tree within it we already have 11×11 spheres without multiplying this by a further 4!

At first we may wonder what is the value of splitting the Tree into four worlds. When we start relating these worlds to other maps and concepts of consciousness, however, it becomes clearer. We find in many different systems there is a division into four, such as the four 'elements of the wise' from alchemy: fire, water, air and earth. The First World relates to the creative fire, the second to the receptive water, the third to the formative air and the fourth to the material earth. Sometimes there is said to be a fifth element, Spirit, which is the breath of the Creator giving life to all the worlds.

If we look at the four worlds as progressive layers or veils which temper the light of the original creation, we can understand the underlying intention. For the physical world to exist and be populated by all the different beings, including humans, the original creative spark had to be kept aflame but veiled in such a way that it would not be too bright or blinding for the created beings. The first world is therefore seen as that of pure Spirit and, being associated with fire, can be seen clearly as something too powerful on its own to fulfil the function of creation. The second world of water is created to balance the fire. Once this is done it allows further creation to proceed, but for this formative energy to move into manifestation it has to be infused with the breath of the creator. Air is the obvious medium for this. The fourth material world of the element of earth can then come into being.

It is said that the Creator wants us to experience the pure qualities of soul in the fullest sense. The Creator progressively veiled its energies so we could gradually but surely move back towards our source without being burnt up by too great an energy. Perhaps some of the people who in our society are deemed 'mad' or 'psychotic' have opened up to these energies too soon and have been 'burnt' by the creative fire. Whether this is the case or not, it certainly acts as a reminder to us to work at our own pace and, when necessary, to seek guidance from those who are already travelling the path.

We saw in an earlier chapter how in Genesis, what is normally translated as 'God' in the original Hebrew is ELO-HIM, the Mother-Father Creator. When we reach Exodus, where the actual physical manifestation takes place, the word usually translated as 'God' is in Hebrew IHVH, Jehovah. It is sometimes said that this is the unspeakable name of 'God' and that if it is pronounced correctly the whole universe will cease to exist. For this reason, Jewish people often will not say Jehovah when they meet this word in the Bible but replace it with Adonai, a name for the personal 'god' within each of us. IHVH is seen by Qabalists, however, as more than just an unpronounceable name of 'God'. It is seen as the key formula to understanding the whole of creation.

IHVH, sometimes called Tetragrammaton, is composed, as we can see, of four Hebrew letters, I-H-V-H, yod, heh, vau, heh. These four letters relate, in their given order, to the four worlds as discussed above. Through correspondences we then see that they also relate to the four elements. The four letters are also related to the four parts of a created being – I to the head, H to the shoulders and arms, V to the rest of the trunk and the final H to the legs. If you write these four Hebrew letters (see Appendix for shapes) one directly under the other, you will even see that they pictorially represent a human body.

There are many more mysteries associated with IHVH, most of which are beyond the scope of this book. For instance, I relates to the 'father', H to the 'mother', V to the 'son' and the final H to the 'daughter'. These four are then said to represent force, pattern, activity and form. The force (will or energy) and the pattern (the blueprint or balance) come together, and two equally balanced creations result, the son and daughter. They represent the activity (doing) of the world and the form (or being) of the world. The more we delve into the mysteries of IHVH the more we find that it aids us in realizing the beautiful cosmic pattern described in the Qabalistic vision of creation.

THE FOUR WORLDS OF COLOUR

Each of the four worlds has a particular colour scheme associated with it. These four scales of colour are called the king, queen, emperor and empress scales. For all practical purposes, however, the traditional colours used are those of the queen scale. If you look at the Tree of Life on the front cover of this book you will see that the spheres and paths are coloured following this tradition. It has been found to be effective to use these colours both when we are learning to visualize the Tree and when we are using it for personal growth and healing.

The Supernal Triad of Kether, Chockmah and Binah, with regard to its colouring, indicates the nature of these spheres and the creative act. Kether, the 'divine spark', is white brilliance, white being the 'colour' which absorbs no other colours, but reflects them all out into its surroundings. Binah, the great sea of spiritual love, is black – black being the 'colour' that absorbs and includes all other colours. True spiritual love also absorbs and includes without rejection or judgement. Chockmah, sitting between these two, is then seen as silver grey, a mixture of white and black. Daath, incidentally, the 'sphere without a number', is also sometimes given no colour. In its manifestation, however, it is seen as a 'rainbow bridge' between the Supernals and the rest of the Tree and has thus been coloured accordingly.

It is interesting to observe that the three central spheres (those of 'soul') are coloured with the primary colours, that is, red (Geburah), blue (Chesed) and yellow (Tiphareth). The colours of the three personality spheres are combinations of the primary colours. Netzach is green (a mix of Chesed and Tiphareth, blue and yellow), Hod is orange (mixing the colours of Geburah and Tiphareth), whilst Yesod is purple (mixing the colours of Geburah and Chesed).

Malkuth was traditionally coloured with russet, citrine, olive and black to represent the four elements. As the elements are more usefully seen to correspond to different spheres and worlds on the Tree, this has been changed. Perhaps the most obvious colours for the earth might at first be thought to be green or brown, but when we work with Malkuth energies we find that a light, sky-blue colour is most effective. This is not surprising considering the high percentage of the earth's surface which is covered with water, and pictures from space missions confirm the beautiful blue colour of our planet. On a deeper level as well, the energy of our planet (called 'orgone energy' by Wilhelm Reich) is seen as blue.

If we look at the colours and relate them to the four worlds, we see that the first two worlds are involved with the creative and receptive aspects of Creation and thus are shown either to reflect or absorb all colour. The third world, that of Yetzirah and formation, includes the three primary colours and the three colours created when these are mixed together. Assiah, the fourth world of the earth, is coloured in line with our perception of our planet, particularly as it is seen both energetically and from outer space. The coherence of this colouring for the Tree of Life is quite beautiful, and is a good example of the value in understanding Qabalistic correspondences.

ENERGY CENTRES

The different energies we have within our bodies can be understood easily through the Tree of Life. As both Eastern and Western systems attest, there are innumerable 'power points' within us. Eastern systems delineate seven major power points that are called 'chakras' and these correspond to the planes on the Tree of Life. When any of these major power points are opened, they give the individual powers of perception and creativity. The seven major 'chakras', along with their corresponding spheres, are:

energy centre	chakra name	spheres on Tree of Life
base of spine	muladhara	Malkuth
genital	svadisthana	Yesod
solar plexus	manipura	Hod and Netzach
heart	anahata	Tiphareth, Geburah and Chesed
throat	visuddhi	Daath
midhead	ajna	Binah and Chockmah
top of head	sahasrara	Kether

If you consider this table along with diagram 8 you will understand how the Tree of Life fits onto the human body. This is vitally important to understanding the Qabalah, for it

61

is through our bodies that we are able to bring anything into manifestation. There would seem to be little point in accessing deep spiritual realms and having enlightening insights, for example, if we are unable to do something with this in our everyday world.

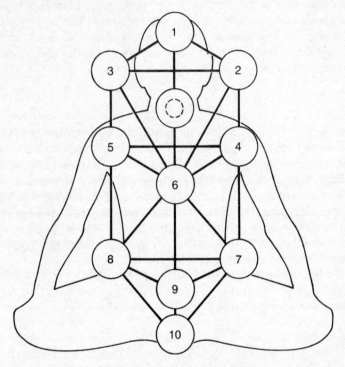

Diagram 8   The Human Body

There are more power points in the body than the seven 'major' ones, and through closely considering our bodies with an imaginary Tree overlaid, we can quite easily find many of them. For example, the places where paths cross one another on the Tree, when related to the body, help us locate precise psycho-spiritual centres of great healing benefit. It is well worth looking at your own body to see if you can find the location of any of these other centres.

The major physical power points or chakras may be seen as 'rotating discs' of energy that, on the level of the energy bodies, are attached to the spine at seven specific points, from the base of the spine up to the very top. If we compare the chakra system to the Tree of Life, we can see that some of the energy centres have more than one sphere corresponding to them. Some of the chakras are concerned with 'external duality', that is they are involved with outer balance, and these have a single sphere associated, the 'other half' of the polarity being outside the individual person. Those concerning 'internal duality' are involved with balance within the individual and have more than one sphere associated.

The solar plexus chakra, corresponding to Hod and Netzach, is dual in nature since the left and right hand sides of the individual have to be balanced for it to be effectively and fully open. In other words, if our thoughts (Hod) and our feelings (Netzach) are not balanced there will be issues to be worked through at this level of energy. The midhead chakra is also dual in nature but on a deeper level as shown by its correspondence to Binah and Chockmah. It is concerned with the balance of spiritual Love and Will and when it is open gives the individual connection to deep spiritual insights.

We will be looking at the heart in relation to the Tree of Life in more depth in a later chapter. The heart chakra primarily relates to the central sphere on the Tree, Tiphareth. It is also associated with Geburah and Chesed, however, as it has a dual aspect that is concerned with the lessons the soul has to learn in its journey through life. A connected and subtly effective heart chooses to open or close as appropriate to the situation at hand, being able to heal itself and others but also able to protect its body, its means of expression. Tiphareth and the heart are associated with 'higher' feelings, values, love, service, altruism, and so on. Humanity as a whole is said to be moving in the current age, from a primary focus on solar plexus issues towards a new connection and awakening of heart values.

The 'single' chakras, with regard to their position on the Tree of Life, are simpler to understand. Whereas with the other chakras the concern is with inner balance, these four chakras are concerned with outer balance. The base of spine chakra

(Malkuth) – survival in the world; sexual chakra (Yesod) – interplay and interpersonal relationships, particularly sexually oriented ones; throat chakra (Daath) – expression and communication, and the crown chakra (Kether) – the realization of unity within and without, and the connection to the Mother-Father Deity.

SOUL, PERSONALITY AND THE WORLD

Most of the time we are so involved with the everyday processes of physical survival, emotional reaction and intellectual fantasy that we have no time to consider anything which might be deemed 'spiritual'. Indeed, many people live their whole lives, albeit undoubtedly touched by the Spirit, without ever considering their deeper nature. If and when such moments arise, therefore, when we find ourselves face to face with our spiritual nature or our 'soul', they are often overpowering, or disturbing in some way. We may be frightened by the experience and choose to cut off, even deny its reality. Even if we enjoy the experience, it is likely that we will get caught up again in the everyday chores of life and lose sight of our connection.

When we consider these moments in our lives we tend to see them in terms of something we have had happen to us. Basically we act as if we are personalities who sometimes have spiritual experiences. We will say, in one way or another, that we 'have a soul'. One of the key concepts in the Qabalah is concerned with reversing this perception of our reality so that we become a soul who has a personality. We are not the lower part of the Tree with something deeper within us. We are encouraged to live our lives with the realization that we are Tiphareth and the higher spheres, we are soul, and to come into manifestation we have clothed ourselves with the personality spheres (Netzach through to Malkuth). This is not just a concept, for we find if we start to believe this and, more importantly, act upon it, our world is transformed. What used to be problems that we were somehow forced to deal with are transformed into opportunities for our development and growth.

Exercise 5: The Soul Cloak

Between the personality spheres on the Tree of Life and Tiphareth is a veil, sometimes called the 'Veil of Paroketh'. This veil acts as a cloak so that until we make our own direct connection to soul energies we are not confused or dazzled by the energies that are then available to us. In the next chapter we will be starting to look at our journey of 'soul-making' using the Tree of Life, so this exercise is intended to prepare us for this work.

Before starting, sit comfortably, relax and focus for a while on your breathing. Do not force or change your breathing in any way, but simply allow your awareness to follow the air as it enters your lungs then is released. If you are breathing in a very shallow way you may want to deepen your breathing a little, but otherwise simply trust in your own breathing pattern. As you watch your breathing, become aware of any particular tensions in your body and choose to let go of these tensions with your out-breath.

Imagine you are wearing a dark, heavy, black cloak. The hood is up and is pulled right over your head, hiding your face. Spend a little while really imagining this cloak, feeling its presence all around your physical form.

This dark, hooded cloak is the cloak of your negativity, your fears and the negative emotions, thoughts and sensations you experience in your life. Really feel the heaviness of this cloak.

Now become aware that this negative cloak is gradually lifting up and away from your body, taking with it all your negativity. Really feel this cloak loosening and lifting away from you.

Imagine the cloak slowly vanishing.

Once it is completely gone, you are free to clothe yourself in a new cloak of your choice, a cloak of love, joy, beauty, protection, or any other quality you choose. Choose the cloak you wish to wear right now.

Vividly imagine yourself wearing the new cloak you have chosen, this cloak of light and positive energy. See its colour and feel its strength and quality all around you.

Realize this new cloak is a symbol for your soul. Realize that as a soul you can wear whatever cloak you choose.

Realize you are a soul and choose wisely.

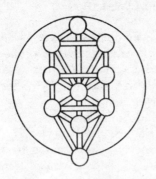

6 · THE WHOLE PERSON

In the light of the Qabalah, the shadows of transitory things are instantly banished.

Aleister Crowley

One of the greatest, and best known, esoteric maxims is: 'as above, so below'. From the viewpoint of the Qabalah this statement asserts the essential identity between the Mother-Father Deity and the Creation. We could say 'god' made man in his own image (and, of course, 'goddess' made woman in her own image). To a Qabalist this is not acceptable, however, because it implies a dualism that denies the theories and the experiences that occur when we connect with our inner world. It would be truer to say 'goddess-god' made 'woman-man' in its own image, then split this creation into two so that, through this division, the creation may experience love and realize its true essential identity with the Deity.

When we consider the triangles that make up the Tree of Life we see that, despite the flipping upside down of the second and third ones, the three triangles are reflections of each other. Qabalists believe this is exactly the case, each triangle successfully clothing itself with denser matter until the world of Malkuth can be formed. Until Malkuth is created, the actual split into male and female does not occur. Despite the way the energy is made denser as it descends the Tree, the essence of the Deity is carried through all the spheres without being lessened or diluted at all. It is true to say, therefore, that the Deity is as equally in Malkuth as in Kether. Thus we return to the maxim, as above, so below.

A similar Qabalistic maxim says, 'Kether is in Malkuth and Malkuth is in Kether. . . .' This clearly implies the same meaning. The Macrocosm (represented by the top triangle) is perfectly reflected in the Microcosm (represented by the bottom triangle). The Qabalistic maxim continues, however, by saying '. . . but after another manner.' In other words, the Deity and the Creation are the same except for a difference! This may sound like a contradiction until we understand what the difference is, namely the knowledge of existence. Once the creation achieves this self-knowledge, therefore, it becomes one with the Deity. This is exactly what Jesus meant when he said, so simply and clearly, 'know thyself'.

For a Qabalist this knowing of oneself has to be a direct experience, not simply a matter of faith. Without denying the importance of faith, it is clear that to have true self-knowledge we must directly experience our own selves. From this experience we may then have a living faith, based on our direct, experienced understanding, which is very different from a 'blind faith' based upon what someone else has told us to be the truth. For some people faith alone might be enough to sustain them and help them develop and grow closer to an understanding of their own inner nature, but the Qabalah stresses that if we are to truly know ourselves as one with the Divine, we must experience this directly.

Everything that a Qabalist experiences is seen as an opportunity for growth and movement towards self-realization. Not least amongst these opportunities are those presented to us through our bodies. The body, represented by Malkuth, is seen as a living temple of the soul. It is through our bodies that we incarnate on this planet, and it is only through our bodies that we can interact with the dense matter of existence. It is vital, therefore, that we treat our bodies with all the respect that is due to such a precious temple.

Malkuth, as you know, also represents the external world and this too is seen as a temple, the outer temple in which we experience and express ourselves. We can thus make another connection, that between our inner temple (body) and outer temple (external world). It is important we treat our outer temple with as much respect as that we give our inner temple. When we abuse our planet, it reflects our abuse of ourselves. When we truly honour our bodies, we inevitably honour our outer temple too.

Whatever we know scientifically, from our planetary perspective we experience the sun as dying each evening and being reborn each morning. If we could stand on the sun, we would realize the light as continuous, at the centre of all activity, including the cycles of the earth. Similarly, from our terrestrial perspective, we experience a similar cycle of life and death. As souls, however, we can realize our continuity, seeing that birth and death are transition points that bring us into and take us out of incarnation on the planet. If we experience this truth, we inevitably see that there is some purpose for coming into incarnation. For a Qabalist this purpose is, in essence, to realize our true inner divinity and connection to the Deity.

For each of us, as individual souls, however, there is, in any incarnation, a particular purpose for being here. We have special lessons to learn, and until we truly experience and understand our lessons, we continue spiralling through an endless cycle of experiences (and incarnations even), with these lessons being presented to us in numerous different ways. Once a particular lesson is learnt, we can then move on to the next lesson. Each step in this unfolding process brings us nearer to the realization of our purpose or 'true will', the reason why we are here. For one person the purpose might be to express love in some lofty, abstract sense, for another to express love in caring for sick or handicapped people. Perhaps for someone else it may be to stand against a particular injustice so more truth can be made manifest, for another it might simply be to act as a catalyst for someone else's progress. No individual's purpose is better or worse than another's. The key is to find our own purpose or true will and then to do it. When we achieve this we have truly aligned ourselves, as souls, with the universal Spirit, and can actualize the identity between the microcosm and the macrocosm.

ARCHETYPES OF EXPERIENCE

The two primary archetypes that mould our experience are 'Love' and 'Will'. These are represented on the Tree of Life by Chesed and Geburah, the two spheres that, together with Tiphareth, form the soul triangle. This is not to say that Love and Will are the same as soul, but through an understanding of correspondences, we can say that the purpose for the soul's incarnation is expressed, in each individual, through their relationship with these two archetypes.

The archetypes of Love and Will manifest in our person-alities in a variety of ways. Very simply, we can say that most people tend to be more developed in their connection to one of these archetypes and relatively under-developed in their connection to the other. Someone who has developed their Geburah, for instance, will tend to be self-determined, have focused awareness and be strong enough to assert themselves appropriately. If the development of Geburah has been at the expense of Chesed (the archetype of Love), they may tend to be manipulative, selfish and ambitious, and have an underlying fear of becoming impotent and powerless. On the other hand, someone who has a well-developed connection to Chesed will tend to be co-operative, sensitive, caring and receptive. If the development of Chesed has been at the expense of Geburah (the archetype of Will), however, they will tend towards attachment, dependency, conformity, and have an underlying fear of loneliness, totally bereft of love.

In either case, whether the imbalance is on the side of Geburah or Chesed, we need to re-balance through bringing the level of the lesser developed archetype up to the level of the more greatly developed one. This way we create a dynamic balance through inclusion. The archetype which has been developed more will also need work done on it, but rather than depressing it, a Qabalist will work actively to refine its distortions. As well as this 'psychological' work, a Qabalist will also work 'magikally' through finding ways of aligning his or her personal connection to Will and Love (as expressed through Geburah and Chesed) to Spiritual Will and Love, which are represented by Chockmah and Binah, the second and third spheres on the Tree of Life.

We can see, by looking at a diagram of the Tree of Life, that personal will is on the left hand column under Spiritual Love and personal love is on the right hand column under Spiritual Will (Purpose). If we see these two planes on the Tree as the bases of the top two triangles, to align the triangles so their correspondences match, we would need not only to invert one of them, we would also have to spiral it round. This spiralling effect shown on the Tree of Life indicates how the connection between the Supernal Triad of the Spirit and the second triangle of soul is not made through simple reflection of the energy, but involves an active spiralling process. We are reminded of the DNA spiral as being a similar key, on another level, to the understanding of the meaning of life.

In our personalities, we find a correlation between Love and Will and 'female' and 'male'. Firstly, it must be stressed that all men and all women have both 'female' and 'male' inside them. A soul that manifests as a man usually manifests a deeper soul connection to the 'feminine' and vice versa. However this may be, we all tend to manifest our connection to Geburah and Chesed through how we learn to relate to our own male and female qualities. We learn much of this from our parents. Generally speaking, a baby views its mother as a living embodiment of Love, its father as a living representation of Will. From the interaction between our parents and between them and us, we start to learn how we are going to manifest our understanding of Love and Will in our current incarnation.

From the Mother-Father Deity right through to the most earthly manifest 'maleness' or 'femaleness', the Qabalah stresses the absolute equality of male and female. If we apply the maxim 'as above, so below' to this, we can see that another aspect of the work for a female Qabalist is to elevate the 'inner male' and to refine the 'outer female'. Correspondingly, for a male Qabalist the work is to elevate the 'inner female' and refine the 'outer male'. This work ensures balance and the subsequent alignment with the soul. It also, of course, aids the work of the soul in its journey towards alignment and integration with the Spiritual Triad. A Qabalist will maintain that this is just one example of how the most mundane, everyday work we perform on our growth and development is no less important than work that appears deeper or loftier. Indeed, just as the 'godname' for Kether, the Spiritual Self, is Eheieh, meaning 'I Am That I Am', a Qabalist affirms in his or her work an essential connection to the Divine and will also say, in moments of true connection and ecstasy, 'I am that I am'.

When we actively participate in the mysteries of the Tree of Life, we are aligning our human imagination with the Divine Imagination. It was this Divine Imagination that the Deity used to create the cosmos. By using our human imagination to work with the Tree, we start to comprehend the Divine Imagination. You may now wonder why we have not yet met an attribution for 'imagination' on the Tree of Life. Quite simply, it is because human imagination and Divine Imagination are always inseparable, and the whole Tree of Life, and all it represents, is the product of this imagination. This is not to say the world is unreal in some way. On the contrary it is a positive affirmation of the Absolute Reality of all creation.

A MULTIPLICITY OF UNITY

We are all divine, not in some abstract sense, but in our everyday lives. Whatever we do, we are never disconnected from our essential nature. The myths of gods and goddesses often show us that even divine beings may stray from their purpose and misdirect their energies. We humans are no different! To realize and, more importantly, to manifest our essential divinity, we have to work at it. This is a life-long process and extreme caution is advised when we meet those who would tell us of their 'great initiations', 'spiritual attainment', 'understanding of the true Qabalah' and so forth. Part of the work of the Qabalah, in showing us our own true nature, is to help us re-own our power from all the 'masters', 'secret chiefs', gurus, shamen and the like. To a Qabalist, everyone met on the path is at least an equal, and always possibly just the person we need to teach us a particular lesson.

As well as being surrounded by this endless multiplicity of other 'divine beings' masquerading as humans, all other entities in all the universes, whether imagined or 'real', are truly aspects of the Divine. A Qabalist is on the look out, therefore, for messages, teachings, understanding, not only from other humans or from some direct spiritual inspiration, but also from archangels, angels, demons, animals, plants and rocks! If this sounds fantastic, consider what it means to view the world this way. Whatever we may believe (consciously), our unconscious carries endless possibilities. If we can connect to this realm of the unconscious, we can liberate energies which can enrich our understanding of ourselves and all our potential. Without choice, we tap into the unconscious every night in our dreams. The Qabalah says how much better to tap into the unconscious as often as possible. Or, indeed, how wonderful to realize that everything in our lives is a manifestation from the unconscious. From this viewpoint it is no less strange or fantastic to talk to an archangel than it is to dream of a goldfish.

The danger with this work is that the practitioner will get carried away in her or his own personal imagination to a degree that becomes dangerously ungrounded. This is why we constantly stress for all Qabalistic work the importance of grounding. All work starts in Malkuth and ends there. If we do not follow this advice we do so at our own peril and can easily fall prey to the glamours of self-delusion and 'self-importance' which lead only to 'self destruction'. This is often described Qabalistically as building a castle on the sands of the Abyss (between the Supernal Triad and the rest of the Tree). However strong a castle it may be, it has lost its connection to the Spirit and, having no ground in Malkuth, its foundations shift with the sands of the Abyss and are doomed to dissolution.

It is also important with all Qabalistic work – and for that matter for all work of self-development whatever the system – to remember the sacredness of all life. Everything has its 'angel', its 'divine breath', from each individual cell through to the planet earth and the whole universe. Everything is interconnected, nothing in our universe is separate (however temporarily separate it may sometimes appear). To be truly divine ourselves, we cannot deny the divinity of any other being, for to do so would deny our own divinity. Qabalists believe that every being is a spark of the divine. As such we all have the right to do what we will, and no one has the right to interfere with another being's will. If what we think is our will does interfere with someone else, then we are not doing our true will.

We have a collective responsibility to the totality of life. Every time we do anything that is thoughtless, uncaring or 'off-mark' in some way, we lessen the total amount of connection and consciousness on our planet. Conversely, every time we do something with care, whenever we act from our true selves, we add to the pool of positive consciousness on our planet. We are all individually responsible, and each act we perform does make a difference. The Tree of Life can aid us in aligning ourselves with the purpose and intention of the Deity, and in becoming true and clear receptacles for the inflow of spiritual and psychic energies. Through the work we do on ourselves, it offers us a connection to our common work of collective responsibility.

MANIFESTING SOUL

In Chapter 10 we will discuss in detail the central importance of the heart in all Qabalistic work. The heart is represented on the Tree of Life by Tiphareth, the sphere in the centre of the diagram numbered six. Tiphareth means 'Beauty' and 'Harmony'. The beauty referred to is that created when everything in our being is synthesized into a complete whole, the harmony is that which results from living from a clearly defined centre. The experience of Tiphareth, of having a distinct self-consciousness that we can clearly define and separate from the contents of our consciousness, is what distinguishes us from most other living beings.

We do not usually experience pure self-consciousness, however, but instead experience it mixed with and veiled by everything we are sensing, feeling and thinking at any time. We usually live our lives identified with or attached to our personalities. To make our self-consciousness an explicit, experienced fact we need to be able to disattach ourselves from the 'contents' of consciousness. We need to make the 'flip over' referred to in the last chapter where we become a soul with a personality rather than a personality with a soul.

Through deliberate dis-identification from the personality and identification with the soul, we gain freedom and the power of choice to be identified with or dis-identified from any aspect of our personality according to what is appropriate for any given situation. Thus we may learn to utilize our whole personality in an inclusive and harmonious way. When we do this, we are manifesting our soul energy, not in some exclusive, 'pure' way, as if it is something 'out there', but directly through being exactly who we are at any given moment.

We have already seen how Qabalists stress the importance of 'grounding', of bringing all insights, experiences, spiritual connections, soul energies, inspiration and so on into manifestation. We continually return to two questions: what is the point of coming into incarnation if we are going to spend our time here attempting to separate from or 'transcend' the earth in some way? And what is the point of having a spiritual insight or connection if it remains ungrounded, unconnected to the everyday flow of energy on our planet?

If we believe, as Qabalists do, that the purpose of incarnation is to further the realization of soul in everything which is made manifest, then it is our 'work' to further this realization. We can only do this if we effectively engage ourselves with the world of matter as represented by Malkuth. In other words, we have to connect Tiphareth to the earth. To do this effectively, we have to:

– banish all other ideas apart from the matter at hand, be one-pointed in Hod (representing our thinking function);

– purify our feelings, be clear and connected in Netzach (representing our feeling function);

– consecrate ourselves to the work of incarnation, dedicating ourselves to the single purpose of manifesting Tiphareth (in this sense representing our experience of soul through our intuitive function);

– ground ourselves in direct relationship to the earth, bringing our inner connections into clear manifestation in Malkuth (representing our sensing function, our bodies as a whole, and the physical world).

Sometimes we cannot achieve these aims, perhaps because we lack the will to do it, we become distracted, we devalue our own importance, or we inflate our importance out of all proportion. Fear can also get in the way of clearly manifesting soul energies – fear of the responsibility involved, of losing our individuality, of misusing power, of inadequacy, loneliness, of being rejected, of being 'wrong' in some way, and so on. By thoroughly connecting ourselves to the Tree of Life and continuously grounding our work in Malkuth, however, we may achieve our aims in a centred and grounded way. The following exercise offers us the opportunity of receiving a 'gift' from the soul and then to find ways of using this gift in the world.

Exercise 6: A Gift to Ground

Make yourself comfortable, relax and take a few deep breaths. As you breathe out, let go of any nagging tensions in your body, and as you breathe in, be aware that you are breathing in life-giving energy.

Close your eyes and imagine you are standing on a windswept moor. Take some time to imagine this place as clearly as you can. Fill in as much detail as possible – what can you see around you? What can you smell, hear, taste on the wind? Is it raining lightly or with wind-swept gushes of rain that beat against your body? How do you feel? What are you wearing? Really allow yourself to get a sense of being alone on this windswept moor.

As you look around you, see in the near distance a solitary standing stone. Start walking in the direction of this stone, staying connected to the feeling of being alone on the windy moor.

Just as you reach the stone, there is an opening in the clouds above and a ray of light shines onto the stone, illuminating it clearly. Lying atop the stone is a small object, a gift left here for you by an angel. Don't try and work out what this gift may be, but without judgement or censorship, see what the gift actually is. In your own time, pick up the gift, hold it tightly in your hands, then thank the angel for leaving it for you.

Return to your everyday consciousness, back in the room where you started, bringing the gift with you. You may like to spend a little while now writing about this experience and describing the gift, or drawing a picture of it. Consider your gift in detail – what is it? What does it mean to you? You may not know what the gift is, or what it is for, but trust it was the right gift for you to receive at this time. If you stay attached to it, and remain conscious of it, its meaning will become clearer.

Whether you understand the meaning of your gift or not, the most important action for you now is to find some way to manifest this gift in Malkuth. Maybe there is some action you can take to ground this gift symbolically. For instance, if your gift was a red heart, to ground it perhaps you need to express your love to someone. Perhaps you received a precious jewel and you need to acquire such a jewel in 'real life'. Maybe all you need to do to ground your gift is to remain aware of it and let its energy infuse your actions. You have to find your own way of grounding your gift for in so doing you will bring some soul energy into manifestation on the earth. You are then participating in the most important work for a Qabalist, making a direct link between Tiphareth and Malkuth.

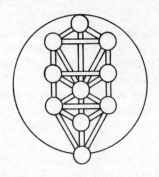

7 · WAYS OF ACTION

The thirty-two mystical paths of the concealed glory are ways of life, and those who want to unravel their secrets must tread them.

Dion Fortune

We can see the whole of life as a journey. We are born out of a state of undifferentiated unity then we walk the path of life, becoming more and more differentiated, more individually ourselves. As we learn to integrate our experiences and realize our potential, we move towards a new unity, more of a chosen union. Finally, we reach the end of our journey and step into death, consciously or unconsciously, willingly or unwillingly. Wherever our life journey takes us we will die, of that we can be certain. In looking at an individual life as a journey, we can ignore what may have come before and what may come after. As interesting and important as these subjects are, in themselves they do not consciously figure as part of the journey. Of course, our attitudes and beliefs about these matters will affect how we tread our path.

Just as we tread the path of our life journey towards our end in death, so we can similarly see different parts and areas of our life as little journeys within the larger life journey. For example, adolescence can be seen as a journey from childhood towards adulthood; education is a journey towards greater knowledge; marriage a shared journey of discovery, and so on. A single day in our life can be viewed as a journey, from awakening back to sleep, and within any single day we will make many even smaller journeys. Even in reading this book you make numerous journeys from one paragraph to the next.

Whether our journeys are internal or external ones, whether they are long and complicated or short and simple, whether they are pursued singly or whether we are travelling many journeys at once, we are always stepping along pathways from somewhere to somewhere else. Looked at this way we can say that each step on every path is as significant as every other step. Further, the most important step is always the next step, for without making the next step we do not journey forwards. This may sound very obvious, but much of the time most of us live without this awareness. We look forward to our goal, missing many individual steps on the way, sometimes even stepping onto a completely different path than we intended. We look backwards, congratulating ourselves or worrying over some steps we have already made, perhaps wishing we could change them. We generally find it very difficult to focus on our current path and the next step we have to make to carry us forwards.

If we apply this understanding to our work with the Tree of Life we can see two clear principles emerging. Firstly, that we are travelling on the paths of the Tree at all times, even though we may not always be aware of where we are on the Tree. Secondly, the most important step for us to take is the next, so we are well advised to concentrate on that step before worrying about others we may need to take later. In this book we have already spoken of the twenty-two paths that connect the ten spheres on the Tree of Life. Traditionally the spheres are also called 'paths', so in this context it is said there are thirty-two paths on the Tree. As the Tree of Life is a map of our consciousness, the more clearly we become aware of where we are on the Tree (that is, in our lives), the more effectively we can experience the world and express ourselves appropriately.

'Pathworking' is a term used quite frequently these days to describe any kind of 'guided fantasy' or 'directed day-dreaming', whether it involves the Qabalah or not. For a Qabalist the term refers to making a connection with one or more of the 'thirty-two paths' on the Tree of Life. Beyond that, it can be applied to any method for making such connections, from formal rituals through to simple realizations of the need to make psychological connections. For instance, if I knew that I needed to balance my feeling and thinking functions, I would do work with the path that connects Hod and Netzach, for this is the path relating to the relationship between these two functions.

More often than not, when people speak of pathworking with the Tree of Life they are referring to the setting up of complex 'stories' that can be used to direct the imagination of the aspirant through the required paths to a particular goal. We might decide, for instance, to travel up the Middle Pillar to Tiphareth, passing through the path connecting Malkuth to Yesod, Yesod itself, then the path from Yesod to Tiphareth. Our 'guiding fantasy' would incorporate symbols and images that correspond to these paths. The following table shows some of the simplest correspondences to these paths, but of course there are many more. Quite complex tables of such correspondences can be found in *The Living Qabalah* (see Further Reading).

Path	10 to 9	Yesod	9 to 6	Tiphareth
Hebrew letter	tau		samekh	
astrology	saturn	moon	sagittarius	sun
colour	black	purple	yellow	gold
tarot	universe	four '9's	art	four '6's
stones	onyx	quartz	topaz	diamond
perfumes	lavender	jasmine	hyacinth	frankincen
flowers	nightshade	iris	rose	gorse
animals	crocodile	hare/cat	horse/dog	lion/spider
herbs	rue	watercress	bay	rosemary
Greek deity	Athena	Zeus	Artemis	Helios
Roman deity	Saturn	Hecate	Diana	Apollo

Using these and similar correspondences we could create a story of a journey that incorporates some of these images and

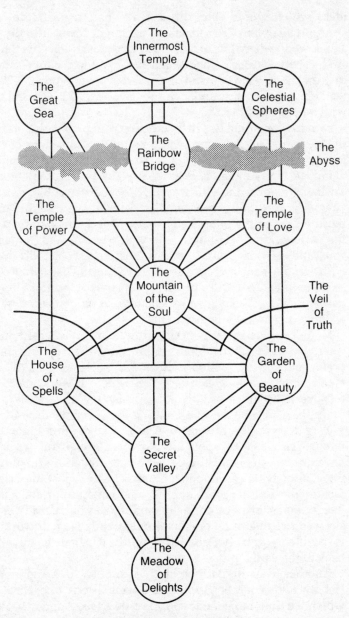

Diagram 9   Pathworking

ideas which would then direct our consciousness into the appropriate sphere. For instance, we might travel initially to a dark wood where lots of nightshade grows and imagine that a strange being with a crocodile-like face gives us a potion of rue to drink; then we may travel on past a purple-hued pool where watercress grows in abundance and have a magickal encounter with a hare; and so on.

Perhaps you might like to try creating your own pathworking in this way. The first step would be to write the story of the journey as suggested in the last paragraph. Include as much detail as you can, and write clearly in the present tense. To then perform the pathworking you have written, centre yourself, close your eyes and let the story guide you into these other realms of consciousness. You might like to tape the pathworking, reading the story slowly and with suitable gaps, and use this to guide you. Alternatively, you could share with a friend, each taking a turn at travelling the path involved. Exercise 6 at the end of the last chapter is a form of simple pathworking and may give you some good pointers on how to effectively perform a pathworking.

Many people use pathworking simply in this way, although generally it is considered more effective to do some preliminary work which will 'raise energy'. This might entail creating a magickal circle in which to work, dancing to raise consciousness, invoking protecting archangels and so forth. The essence of the work, however, is to achieve a state where we are receptive to the suggestions that the pathworking makes upon us. If we are successful we will have an experience of the paths we are travelling including relevant insights and understanding. The two most important factors are that the work should be done appropriately, not just for amusement or curiosity, and that, as has already been stressed, we re-ground ourselves in Malkuth. No pathworking is complete – or truly Qabalistic – unless it brings the traveller back to the earth.

Another way of pathworking is simply to imagine the Hebrew letters or other appropriate symbols on a door through which we then project our consciousness (see Appendix 1 for the Hebrew Letters). If you wanted to travel the path from

Malkuth to Netzach, for instance, you would imagine a suitable door with the letter 'Qoph' brightly emblazoned upon it, then imagine that you open the door and pass into the world behind. Whatever you imagine is then your experience of that path. You would finish this work by coming back out of the door and closing it firmly shut. This type of pathworking is much less structured than those where all the symbols are pre-arranged. This way is often more effective, for each individual makes connections with his or her own inner world of symbols rather than trying to impose symbols that may not have that much relevance. For example, if we don't relate at all to crocodiles and, for us, a bull is a better animal to attribute to the path from Malkuth to Yesod, then it is better for us to be honest to our own inner world of symbols than try to fit ourselves into something to which we do not relate.

We can also travel on the paths of the Tree of Life in as many other ways as our own imagination and genius suggest is appropriate for us at any particular time. Diagram 9 shows 'location names' on the Tree which can be used along with the Hebrew letters, for instance, to create quite complex feats of 'imaginary' travel. Later in this chapter, pathworking which involves dancing on the Tree of Life is discussed. This is a quite innovative way of using the energies raised through dancing, combined with appropriate symbols, sounds and movements, to travel on the Tree of Life or, in other words, to connect with various layers of our inner world.

Magick has been defined as the 'science and art of causing willed change to occur'. In other words whenever we do anything from choice and it causes a change, we are doing magick. If we want a certain book, go to a shop and exchange a token (money) for this book, then we have performed an act of magick. If we do a pathworking and understand a little more about ourselves, we have similarly performed an act of magick. The Qabalistic way is a way of magick and, as with all true magick, it has the ultimate aim of manifesting more love and understanding in the universe. When we use our Qabalistic knowledge and understanding wisely, we perform many magickal acts and, through these, partake of the greatest magickal act of all, the complete re-manifestation of Eden on

earth in which all women and men freely and equally partake
of the richness and splendour of life.

TAROT IMAGES AND THE TREE

There are seventy-eight cards in a full Tarot pack, four suits
of ten each, called the minor Arcana, sixteen 'court cards'
and twenty-two 'Major Arcana', 'Atus' or 'trumps'. Diagram
1 shows the attribution of the 'Major Arcana' onto the Tree
of Life. I recommend you study this diagram whilst reading
this section. The origins of the Tarot cards and the Qabalah
seem strangely interwoven, certainly in 'mythical history' if
not in the mundane. The seventy-eight cards of the Tarot
may be assigned to the spheres and paths on the Tree
in a very straightforward and easy to understand manner.
Thus they become very useful 'compendiums' of symbols
for pathworking on the Tree of Life.

Different Tarot designs will more or less agree with the
Qabalistic correspondences, but all Tarot cards, of whatever
design, can be related to the Tree. Some Tarot packs, however,
are more appropriate because they have been deliberately
designed with the Tree of Life in mind. The Thoth Tarot Cards
(see Further Reading) convey the greatest understanding of the
Qabalah and also happen to be amongst the most beautifully
designed cards. Because of this, they can act as very suitable
images for pathworking. We might, for instance, instead of
imagining a door with a Hebrew letter, imagine a curtain on
which is the Tarot symbol, or simply project ourselves into the
world depicted in the design.

The twenty-two paths exactly correspond with the twenty-
two Trumps as already stated. Although different Qabalistic
authorities do not necessarily agree on the attribution of
every card to each path, as you become more familiar with
the Qabalah and the Tarot you will see that the connections
between the ten spheres and the cards are quite self-evident.
The ten spheres of the Tree are also ideally suited for the
attribution of the 'minor cards' of the Tarot which, numbered
1 to 10 in four suits, exactly correspond with the spheres. The
four suits – wands, cups, swords and discs – then relate to the

four Qabalistic worlds, so the whole scheme of the Tree is represented.

On a more material level we can see that the whole seventy-eight Tarot card pack represents the innermost nature of our being and corresponds exactly with the Tree of Life. The essence of this knowledge is gleaned through the 'trumps' which are able to take you into, out of and beyond the Tree and its pathways. The 'Moon' trump, for instance, represents your travels, back and forth, on the path between Malkuth and Netzach.

The 'court cards' of the Tarot relate to the four worlds, the knights (or kings) to the first, creative world, the queens to the second, receptive world, the princes to the third, formative world and the princesses to the fourth, material world of manifestation. The court cards represent how different types of people interact with the Tree of Life. Each person has all these 'types' within them, but some predominate and it is with these 'types' that we are usually associated. If you are a basically creative person who tends to be a bit 'up in the air', the Prince of Wands may be your predominant card, and so on.

The 'small cards' of the Tarot represent the energy of the spheres of the Tree themselves, and the particular aspect of life they convey to us. Through combining their Qabalistic attributions with their astrological correspondences, we can even give these cards fairly meaningful titles. Thus, for example, the six of discs (Tiphareth, the heart, expressed in the material world, sun in Taurus) is called 'Success'; the ten of discs (corresponding to Malkuth and the material world, mercury in Virgo) is called 'Wealth'.

The perfection of this attribution of the Tarot cards to the Tree of Life is quite astounding. As an example, consider the four '4's in a Tarot pack. Because they are numbered four they relate to Chesed, love. The four of wands corresponds to the first world and therefore the element of fire; the four of cups to the second world and the element of water; the four of swords to the third world and the element of air; and the four of discs to the fourth world and the element of earth. The four of wands is therefore the fiery, creative part of Love, the four of cups the watery, receptive part of Love, the four of swords the airy, formative part of Love and the four of discs the earthly, material part of Love.

The ace of each suit, corresponding to Kether, is the pure form of that energy, so for example, the ace of wands is pure creative energy. Each card then represents a progressive degradation of this energy until the ten, which is its most material form, is reached. The ten of wands represents the complete manifestation of creativity. This journey, from the ace to the ten in each suit, is a move from 'potential' energy to 'kinetic' energy. The six represents energy in its 'ideal' balanced form, and the ten, as well as representing its complete manifestation, also includes the seed of decay into the next suit.

QABALISTIC RITUAL DANCE

Through ritual dance we can by-pass our everyday states of consciousness and bring ourselves closer to Tiphareth where we co-operate with rather than resist the unfolding of our inner processes. Our habitual inner dialogue of unfocused chatter in Hod and our emotional reactions from Netzach and Yesod can be turned off. No longer controlled by our personality spheres, we are open to enter the realm of soul. When we dance in this way, we are using our abilities to focus and move to enter altered states of consciousness We can then release energies from Yesod, and use these energies to clear our current consciousness. From the realm of soul we can gain a knowledge and understanding of our potential – in other words we can divine our future possibilities.

Ritual dance is one of the oldest forms of dance, yet how easy it is to miss the relevance of ritual when we see it as something obscure, strange or even frightening. We all perform rituals every day in our lives – from the rituals of rising in the morning through to the rituals of going to bed at night. If we make our rituals conscious then we empower ourselves. We give ourselves the opportunity to change and restructure our daily life rituals so they serve rather than hinder us. Performing our own rituals through which we connect to our body offers us such an opportunity. We can become connected to our soul energy and root this directly onto the earth, Malkuth.

To create Qabalistic ritual dances is not difficult; they do not require the learning of any particular dance or life skills. All you have to do is choose to bring consciousness into your dance, and in your dancing connect with various Qabalistic correspondences. For instance, we can create a simple Qabalistic ritual dance through the correspondences of the four elements of fire, water, air and earth onto the Tree of Life. People used to believe that everything is composed of these four elements in different combinations. So, for instance, a cloud is fiery in its ability to become a storm, watery in its composition and when it rains, airy in its movement, and earthy when it clings to mountains or becomes a low mist.

There are various different ways to attribute the elements onto the Tree of Life. Perhaps the simplest, and most useful to us here, is shown in the following table, which also shows how we can apply the four elements to some aspects of the human being.

Fire	Water	Air	Earth
Netzach	Yesod	Hod	Malkuth
feelings	emotions	thoughts	senses
sight	taste	smell	touch
heart/solar plexus	belly/lower abdomen	head/shoulders	legs, feet/arms, hands

As can be seen from this table, the correspondences give us the basis for creating a dance, one in which we pay attention to our feelings, emotions, thoughts and senses. Through connecting with different aspects of all the elements, you can balance your inner world. Incidentally, in case you were wondering what happened to the fifth sense of 'hearing' in the table above, it is connected to what is sometimes called 'the fifth element' – that of Spirit. So when you use your ears to attune yourself to any music you may choose for your rituals, you are invoking Spirit!

If we create a ritual dance that incorporates the four

elements, taking us through the four lower spheres on the Tree, our aim is twofold. The first aim, as stated, is to create a state of inner balance. We may, for instance, do four separate dances, using earth, air, water and fire to connect us symbolically to these elements. As we do our 'dance of the four elements' it is important to be aware of our sensory world, to stay tuned in and really pay attention to what we are sensing.

The second aim is to lead us towards Tiphareth, where we can connect with our soul energies. After balancing ourselves with the four elements, therefore, we can then create a dance that helps us transcend our attachment with these lower spheres and reach Tiphareth or centred consciousness. The best way to do this is to 'dance until we drop', holding our intention clearly as we do this. If we dance as long and as hard as we can, we can break through the veil of Paroketh, which separates Tiphareth from the lower spheres on the Tree of Life. When we cannot dance any more, we allow ourselves to drop to the floor, at least figuratively. Breathing deeply, we can then focus on how we feel and our expectation of being reborn in Tiphareth. When we have recovered our breath, we rise to our feet and do a 'dance of awakening', expressing our joy at having entered the realm of the soul. If we have successfully transcended our everyday consciousness, we will find ourselves connected to Tiphareth.

When we connect to our centre in this way, we can really let ourselves express our link with all the different Qualities we may express through our souls – joy, love, beauty, truth, honesty, trust, intuition, and so on. As we dance, we can become aware of the 'cup of receptivity' within ourselves. Doing this, we gain insights and understanding about our purpose or 'true will' for being incarnated on the planet at this time. Finally, as with all Qabalistic working we will do a final dance to express this connection and bring us back to Malkuth. All work ends with grounding.

Diagram 10 shows how our Qabalistic Ritual Dance fits onto the Tree of Life. The single line represents our dancing of the four elements through the four lower spheres. It depicts the wand of intention. The circle represents our consciousness, centred in Tiphareth and radiating soul energies into our being. As a circle it depicts the cup of receptivity. It also passes through Chesed, Geburah, Netzach and Hod, thus symbolically linking the archetypes of Love and Will to our feeling and thinking functions. The heart then represents our re-connection with the ground, bringing the heart energy from Tiphareth into our everyday lives. As a heart it depicts the essential element of all Qabalistic work, that of bringing more love into manifestation. We will develop this theme in the last chapter of this book. The heart (in diagram 10) starts in Tiphareth, passes through Netzach and Hod then ends in Malkuth. This symbolically indicates how we can use our mind, feelings and body to ground our work.

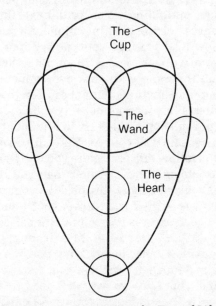

Diagram 10   Dancing on the Tree of Life

When we dance the 'wand of intention', 'cup of receptivity' and 'heart of connection' in this way, we connect to a basic yet vital Qabalistic trinity which helps us bring a balance of Will (intention), and Love (receptivity) into our world.

Exercise 7: Creating a Sacred Space

You have now learned enough Qabalah to be able to construct your own exercise to dance ritually on the Tree of Life. You can make it as complicated or as simple as you wish, and your dance could last anything from half an hour or so to a whole day. Indeed, in one sense, Qabalists spend their whole lives dancing on the Tree of Life!

It is important to feel comfortable both in your inner and outer world for a Qabalistic ritual of any kind to work most effectively. To create an outer 'temple' or sacred space in which to work, the first act is to consecrate the room to your intention. You might like to do this through lighting candles and/or incense, sprinkling water, or through simply walking around the space voicing your intention for its use.

You are now ready to find your 'power spot' in the room where you are working. Focus in on your heart and start moving round the room with your eyes sufficiently open so as not to bump into anything but not so open that you can see objects and items in your room clearly. Don't try to work out where your power spot is, don't try to find it but instead let it find you. There is no way you can rationally discover a power spot, but if you follow this procedure you will find somewhere in your room where you feel better than you do elsewhere. Trust this feeling and choose this place as your power spot.

When you have located your power spot, you might like to do a little dance to express it as yours. Animals have a natural tendency to do this – we have all seen dogs, for instance, turning round a few times before lying down. Your body has the same 'animal instincts', so when you dance in your sacred space trust that your body knows what needs to be done.

Your dance will be aided by the use of suitable music. If you can create your own, so much the better. Drumming, for instance, is always effective in rituals. Alternatively you can choose suitable recorded music to play – something rhythmic and uplifting for dancing in your sacred space, for example. Personally I find instrumental music most effective, but whether you choose classical, rock, jazz, hiphop or acid house music, the selection of suitable music can help you to focus your intention. It can also be great fun to devise musical accompaniment when you are dancing for a specific purpose. Try not to make this an intellectual pursuit, however – you can trust your body to tell you what music moves you most appropriately for any task!

To create an inner 'temple' or sacred space, centre yourself in any way you know, and pay attention to your breathing, initially keeping it deep and slow but without forcing it in any way. You can then sanctify your sacred space through doing a simple 'warm up' dance which expresses your intention. Use any movements or gestures that connect with your intention for creating a sacred space, and if any words or sounds come to you, let yourself express them freely.

Remaining centred, focus on your heart once more and make a series of at least three ritual prostrations. Each time you prostrate yourself, give yourself permission to go right down to the floor, lying on your belly and feeling the ground beneath you. Your first prostration is to thank 'mother earth' for supporting you. Inwardly voice your thanks. Your second prostration is to affirm your awareness and choice in embarking upon whatever work you will do in this room you have sanctified. On the third (and any subsequent) prostration be aware of your specific intention for the work at hand. Be aware that in prostrating yourself to the earth you can affirm not only the sanctity of your work but also the sanctity of all life on our planet.

Finally, silently meditate in your power spot, aware of the sacred energies in both your inner and outer temples. The processes you have just undertaken will have affirmed your place in Malkuth. You are now ready to commence your ritual dance or any other ritual work you wish to undertake.

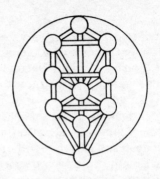

8 · WAYS OF STILLNESS

The crucial notion is that through calming the whirl of thoughts that is our ordinary mind, we open a door that leads to an exalted awareness of the wonder of the entire cosmos.

Edward Hoffman

In the last chapter we were looking at 'ways of action', using pathworking and dance to connect with the Tree of Life and utilize its guidance in our lives. In this chapter we are concentrating on 'ways of stillness', particularly meditation, contemplation and prayer. The aim of both ways of action and stillness is to connect with the deeper or 'higher' aspects of ourselves and find ways of manifesting this energy and understanding into our everyday lives. In Qabalistic work we do not wish to simply 'bliss out', to transcend the mundane and leave the material world behind. On the contrary, our aim is always to clarify our union with spiritual realms and then express this in our lives.

Of course, sometimes just touching the deeper aspects of our nature can in itself be enough. For some people prayer or contemplation is so nourishing and spiritually enriching in itself they feel no need to express their connection. But even when this is the case, it is still true that the link made with these energies may bring better human relations into manifestation, for if we are connecting to spiritual energies we radiate these out to other people and the planet in general. It is inevitable that if we, as individuals, transform ourselves in some way, that transformation will affect those with whom we come into contact.

Many different meanings are given to the word meditation, and there are many different types of meditation and meditative techniques. The word is often used interchangeably with contemplation, then contemplation is used as an alternative word for prayer. Meditation is not the same as prayer, however, although there are many similarities. We will look at prayer and contemplation later in this chapter, but let us first look in more depth at the subject of meditation.

At the simplest level if we concentrate on something – anything at all – we are meditating. The more we learn to control our 'personality functions' as represented by Hod, Netzach and Malkuth and stop them from intruding upon our concentration, the more deeply we enter the meditative state. In fact, many spiritual disciplines – the Qabalah amongst them – consider this work to be of primary importance.

It is often believed that meditation is primarily an abstract activity, involved with turning inwards and somehow transcending the 'ordinary world' of Malkuth. Meditation does involve concentration, reflection, understanding and being receptive. It also includes, however, ways of bringing these connections into outer expression and it is therefore also a very active and outer-directed technique. In this sense, meditation could be defined as the conscious and deliberate use of inner powers and energies to fulfil a specific purpose.

The first action in most types of meditation is to still ourselves in some way. To achieve this physically, to still our Malkuth connection in other words, we might sit in a particular posture and slow down our breathing. Although in Yoga there are many postures all with different meanings and purposes, for simple meditation the key is to find a posture which suits you and stick to it. Then to calm our thoughts and feelings – our Hod and Netzach connections – we have to shift our attention from its normal outer orientation towards the stillness of our inner world. To do this effectively we have to enter a state of emotional peace and direct our thoughts to either stop or be one-pointed. The 'meditation for inner peace' exercise at the end of this chapter has this purpose, and as well as being a complete meditative practice in its own right, can also be used as an opening exercise for all kinds of meditation.

In essence, whatever methods or techniques we choose to use, the aim is to 'turn off the inner dialogue'. This inner dialogue is what is naturally occuring all the time within our consciousness. I feel something and then I think something about it, I hurt my arm and I feel pain, I react to your unkind words then I plot my revenge ... and so on. It is as if we have little 'sub-personalities' within us that are composed of various combinations of our Hod, Netzach and Malkuth functions, and these sub-personalities are all affected by what we carry from our past in Yesod. For instance, one sub-personality might be primarily rooted in Hod and will therefore process any experience in terms of the intellect. It will tend to think things through, be rational, make decisions based on 'sensible solutions' and so on. Another sub-personality might be rooted primarily in Netzach, process experiences in terms of what it feels about them, react non-rationally and make decisions based on 'what feels right'.

These sub-personalities need not be in conflict – either because at their own level they come to some kind of an agreement, or because we learn to view them from a separate, deeper perspective. This perspective is attained in Tiphareth, from where we can witness and direct our actions more clearly. But because most of the time, whether in conflict or not, our sub-personalities keep up a constant chatter inside us, they block our access to inner silence. We have to reach this inner silence, in order to make our prayers and meditation effective, and to be connected to our soul energies, represented on The Tree of Life by the central triangle of spheres. Thus the importance of 'turning off the inner dialogue'.

The Qabalah offers us a map of our awareness that, once we learn to use it, can aid us in silencing the 'chattering' voices of our sub-personalities and come to a deep connection with aspects of our inner nature. Beyond this, it also offers us a map of our spiritual nature that, once we have reached a place of silence, we can then use to understand our subsequent experiences. After turning off our inner dialogue, we see ourselves and our world in a new light. We have entered the realms of the Spirit and soul as represented on the Tree of Life by Tiphareth and above.

A major purpose of all personal and spiritual growth is to connect with our soul and this is clearly the central aim of the Qabalah. Meditation, prayer and contemplation offer us a way towards this goal. However we choose to meditate or pray, it is important that we remember this central aim and do not become distracted by side-issues that can lead us away from our path. The ways of stillness – like the ways of action – are techniques that aid us on our journey, not goals in themselves.

PRAYER AND THE QABALAH

Qabalists believe that one of the simplest and quickest ways to connect with the deeper levels of our being is through prayer. Qabalistic prayer, like meditation, however, is not simply a passive process, but involves active participation. To reach the deep states of connection that are possible through prayer it is important that we engage our whole being, not suppressing any aspect of ourselves. For this reason, during the opening stages of prayer, Qabalists may move their bodies, often in a swaying motion, and willingly speak out any passing emotions or thoughts. The idea of this is to activate the energy of the whole being during the opening stages of the contemplation. Of course there are times when it is appropriate to sit perfectly still and to remain silent, but it is important to stress that this is not the only way to pray, and if we do not allow out the thoughts, feelings and sensations that intrude at the beginning of our prayer, they are very likely to intrude upon us at a later stage.

Once we have engaged our whole personality in the process of prayer, we are then able to proceed to the next step where we go deeper into ourselves. Now we will sit still and not allow any thoughts or feelings to intrude upon our silent concentration. We act as if only the Mother-Father Deity and ourselves exist, and that during this time whilst we are communing with the Deity on a totally personal level, nothing can disturb or distract us.

Prayer is commonly seen as a way of asking for something. We tell 'god' that 'he' is great in some way, we 'confess our sins', 'ask forgiveness', then get down to the real function of saying what we want to happen! Even if what we want to happen is totally altruistic and unselfish, however, Qabalists strongly believe that this is most definitely not the function of prayer. Rather it is to connect us with the deeper or higher aspects of our being and then express this connection in our daily lives. In the process of making this connection we might ask for divine guidance, forgiveness and understanding, but we always remember that this guidance can only come from inside ourselves. If we are inspired this is something inside us. Whether it originates from some abstract, separate 'god' or whether it originates at some deep level of our being ultimately makes no difference. What matters is that we still ourselves so we can hear the message from within then, most importantly, that we live our lives in accord with this.

The Christian Lord's Prayer is a good example of how a simple prayer intended to make a deep and satisfying connection with inner wisdom and understanding can be used in many different ways and for many different aims. However it is used, it is a powerfully invocative prayer, but when we learn the meaning of the original Aramaic words, we find a simplicity and beauty that is missing from the usual translations. A translation of the Aramaic original follows which clearly shows how it is related to the Tree of Life. The usual translation is appended to each line for comparison purposes only.

As you read the Qabalistic Lord's Prayer, consider the Tree of Life. Initially a link is made with the Supernal Triad of Kether, Chockmah and Binah. The creative process instigated in this Spiritual realm is then expressed through the third world of Yetzirah, then grounded in the fourth world of Assiah (Malkuth) with the words 'Grant what we need each day in bread and insight.' The second half of the prayer then ascends the Middle Pillar of the Tree of Life, making a clear connection between the earth and the Spiritual Deity represented by Kether. A final statement closes the prayer and affirms the relevance of this work to our whole being, not just as an abstract or disconnected piece of supplication.

There are different movements and gestures that can be associated with this Qabalistic Lord's Prayer but for now I would recommend that you simply use this prayer as a guide to your Qabalistic studies and as a way of connecting yourself with the energies of the Tree of Life. If you follow the advice regarding contemplation, engage your whole being, then stand upright and voice this prayer, being aware of its relationship to the Tree, you will find it is a very powerful aid to your spiritual development.

Incidentally, Qabalists often use another technique called 'The Qabalistic Cross'. This takes the last phrase of the 'standard' Lord's Prayer, 'For thine is the kingdom, the power and the glory, for ever and ever, amen,' and uses it as a way of focusing consciousness whilst imagining a shining white cross of light and energy on the physical body. It is a very powerful technique and is described in detail in *The Living Qabalah*. The Qabalistic Lord's prayer described next is, however, a more complete contemplative device and can be used to make a deeper connection not only with the form of the Tree of Life but with the force that informs it.

THE QABALISTIC LORD'S PRAYER

Kether: Mother-Father of the Cosmos,
                you create all that moves in light.
                Abwoon d'bashmaya
                (Our father which art in heaven)

Chockmah:	Focus your light within us. *Netqaddash shmakh* (hallowed be thy name)
Binah:	Create your reign of unity now, through our fiery hearts and willing hands. *Teete malkutakh* (Thy kingdom come, thy will be done)
Chesed-Yesod:	Your one desire then acts with ours, as in all light, so in all forms. *Nehvwey tzevyannach aykanna d'bashmaya aph b'arha* (in earth as it is in heaven)
Malkuth:	Grant what we need each day in bread and insight. *Havlan lahma d'sunqanan yaomana* (Give us each day our daily bread)
Malkuth-Yesod:	Loose the cords of mistakes binding us, as we release the ties we hold of others. *Washbwoqlan haubvayn aykana daph hnan shbvoqan l'hayyabayn* (Forgive us our trespasses as we forgive those who sin against us)
Yesod- Tiphareth:	We unite heaven and earth. We fulfil our true purpose. *Wela tahlan le'ynesyuna. Ela patzan min bisha* (For thine is the kingdom)
Tiphareth- Kether:	The power and the love to do, from age to age it renews. *Metul dilakhie malkuta wahayla wateshbuhta l'ahlam almin* (the power and the glory, for ever and ever)
Affirmation:	Sealed in trust and faith, we affirm this with our whole being. Ameyn. Ameyn

ECSTASY AND INNER PEACE

Whenever we pray or meditate, we can distinguish two effects, ecstasy and inner peace. Whilst they are not really separate and usually occur together in some combination or another, it is useful to be aware how we tend to focus on either ecstasy or inner peace. After a connection is made to ecstasy, the usual impetus is to express it outwardly, to share our 'high' with others. After we connect to inner peace, there is a tendency to hold onto it, to feel that outside influences will draw us away from our inner calm. Of course, this is often the case, but Qabalists stress the importance of reversing these typical polarities. When we feel ecstasy, we can choose to draw it into ourselves and use its energies to illuminate and heal our inner world. When we experience inner peace, we can choose to live from this place and radiate our inner harmony into the world.

It is also important not to be goal-orientated in our meditative and contemplative work. If we meditate or pray with the overt intention of becoming more ecstatic or peaceful, our intention in itself can be a block to success. This brings us again to the importance in all developmental work of focusing on the next step. If we are goal-orientated we may miss our step or end up travelling the wrong path altogether. On the other hand, if we connect to our purpose, and then keep our attention on each step we need to make, we will more easily and successfully achieve our aim. If we were going to drive today from, say, London to Manchester, we would need to know where we are going, but to get there we have to pay attention to the road directly ahead of us and successfully negotiate every corner, roundabout, traffic light, and so on. Indeed, in focusing on the path and truly letting go of our attachment to our destination, we may even find we already have the ecstasy and inner peace we desire. The Qabalah stresses that to find these qualities whilst travelling the path is in itself the central aim of all our endeavours.

Exercise 8: Meditation for Inner Peace

This exercise can help you to find inner peace and certainty and to balance yourself, particularly at times of disturbance or low energy. It can also be used at any time as the first step – a tuning in, so to speak – to precede any other Qabalistic or inner work you may be undertaking. Indeed, so powerful is this simple meditation, it cannot really be over-used and the benefits of performing it regularly cannot be overstated.

Find a comfortable posture in which you are relaxed but not so relaxed that you are liable to fall asleep. Pay attention to your breathing, not forcing it, simply watching the rhythmic flow in and out of your body at its natural pace.

After several minutes of simply sitting still and focusing your attention on your breathing affirm silently to yourself: 'My body is at peace.'

Be aware of any sensations in your body – do not try to suppress them in any way, but do not become attached to them, either. Simply watch them pass through your consciousness.

Then affirm silently: 'My emotions and feelings are at peace.'

Again, do not try to suppress any emotions that arise, simply be aware of them and let them pass.

Then affirm silently: 'My thoughts are at peace.'

Let any thoughts that arise be noted, but do not become attached to them. Spend a few minutes now watching sensations, emotions, feelings, thoughts, images, insights or anything else that comes into your consciousness. Observe these events without getting caught up or carried away by them.

Visualize your being as perfectly silent and at peace in a perfectly silent and peaceful world.

Affirm silently to yourself: 'I have sensations, emotions, feelings, thoughts, but I, as an individual spark of the Self, am eternally at peace and at one with the universal rhythm.'

Realize the truth of this statement.

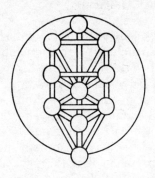

9 · QABALISTIC HEALING

The Tree of Life was impregnated with forces so harmonious and beneficial that its leaves healed every illness and its fruits bestowed eternal life.

Omraam Mikhael Aivanhov

To heal something or someone is to 'make it whole' as indicated by the common root for the words 'heal' and 'whole'. To bring wholeness to something is to complement discord with harmony and pain with wisdom, not to replace or somehow overcome the discord and pain. To be whole does not mean to be perfect in any way, instead it means to include everything. To heal, therefore, is to bring together the component parts of any system – be it a human, animal, plant or 'inanimate' system – in an including rather than excluding way. When we do this we bring about true healing rather than just the kind of 'healing' which is concerned with fixing pain, disguising discord or in some way treating the symptom rather than the cause.

There are many ways of using the Qabalah for healing and in this introductory book we can only overview some of them. The Tree of Life, being a map of the whole person, is an ideal model to use for healing, whether of ourselves or others. A 'whole healing' of any individual will include the whole Tree

– body, personality, soul and Spirit. For the healing to be fully effective, it will also include the relationship of this individual with their external world. This 'whole healing' will also act on many levels, from the physical, through the psychological, to the deepest levels of spiritual connection, dealing on the way with etheric, astral and other 'subtle' energies.

In this chapter we will be focusing on the ways of using the Tree as a healer of energy disorders and imbalances, but it is important to realize that the psychological work we do with the Tree of Life is also a form of healing. Some people object to this approach, suggesting that by working psychotherapeutically with the Qabalah we are reducing it to little more than another kind of psychotherapy. If this was the only work done, these objections might have substance. To be effective in our more abstract, sensitive and spiritual work, however, it is undoubtedly true that we need to be clear vessels for the reception and transmission of the energies engendered by such work. A thorough programme of therapy is one of the most effective ways of becoming such a clear 'vessel'. There are many examples of people in the esoteric and occult world who have not done this necessary preliminary work, and who thus become bloated with spiritual pride, psychologically disturbed, physically incapable and even downright 'crazy'. Their example, if it could be called that, can serve as a potent and timely reminder to those who wish to by-pass this necessary psychological growth and healing.

The Qabalah offers us a sure and certain way of developing all the parts of our being. Malkuth is involved with the senses and the work in this sphere leads to an increase in sensory awareness and connection, improving our ability to 'be in the world' and manifest our True Will or Divine Purpose. Without direct work on our physical temple in Malkuth, we cannot fulfil our function for incarnating.

The work of Yesod involves the clearing out of repressed material and the integration of the resultant energies into the correct sphere. Clearing out the repressed material surrounding this sphere allows our unconscious energies to work more freely and strengthen the other spheres involved. It also aids our sexual balance and power. As Yesod is connected to both our personal and collective past, the psychological and direct healing work we do in this sphere helps release us from the ties that bind us, including those from our past-life emotional identifications.

Hod and Netzach involve the balancing of their polarity, that is the balance of our thinking and feeling functions. This is affected most clearly through allowing the experience and expression of both spheres. The balance we need to achieve between all spheres on the Tree of Life is not a static balance of equality, but a living dynamic balance. To achieve this, we work to increase our contact with the spheres in which we are 'deficient' and refine the energies of the spheres with which we are more 'identified'.

The work of Tiphareth is the building of a strong centre for the directing of the personality, and for the strengthening of our connection to the soul energies represented primarily by Geburah and Chesed. The work of these two spheres, and those higher up the Tree of Life, is then, in practical terms, allowing and experiencing their energies as they emerge, and thoroughly grounding any inspirational spiritual contacts that may be made. To effectively actualize our potential energy, we need a firm base.

SHEKHINAH – GRACE AND BEAUTY

As we saw in an earlier chapter, the Deity in the Qabalistic Tradition is both male and female. The female aspect of the Deity is sometimes called Shekhinah, and her mysteries are central to an understanding of the Qabalah and Qabalistic healing. Shekhinah is essentially sexual in her manifestation. She is said to enter the bed of a couple who are having loving sexual intercourse and bring them the greater depths of ecstasy that such a union can produce. For Qabalists the sexual act is a divine sacrament, and it is said that if sexual union is not achieved on this deep level, it obviates even the highest spiritual attainments. It is believed that a loving sexual act can bring both partners closer to the Deity than any other 'ritual'. Indeed, by coming together with this understanding, a couple may emulate the original creative act of the

Mother–Father Deity, thus again emphasizing the identity between the macrocosmic and microcosmic worlds.

The union of the 'mother' and 'father' aspects of the Deity takes place in Atziluth and Briah, the first two Qabalistic worlds. The third and fourth worlds of Yetzirah and Assiah are then seen as the fruits of their union. The 'father-god' involved here is Eheieh, the primary force of Kether, whilst the 'mother-goddess' is Shekhinah, the essence of Binah who is also, in her manifest form, seen as the indwelling spiritual presence of the created world in Malkuth. Recall the maxim 'Kether is in Malkuth and Malkuth is in Kether, but after another manner'. For those familiar with Tantra, it is clear that Shekhinah is equivalent to Shakti, thus she is to Eheieh what Shakti is to Shiva.

At the moment of orgasm, Shekhinah, sometimes known as the Holy Spirit, comes into the participants. The female partner may identify with this Spirit whilst the male partner may take her within himself. They are both then able to use the presence of Shekhinah to clarify their energies and make them fit vessels for further spiritual and material work. This is an essential aspect of our healing, for by coming together sexually we may bring a new wholeness to our lives.

The third world of Yetzirah is particularly affected by such work. Inner balance is achieved both on the level of Hod and Netzach (thoughts and feelings) and Geburah and Chesed (Will and Love). Outer balance is increased through the heightening of our energies in Yesod (the sexual centre in the human body), and also the throat (represented on the Tree by the unnumbered sphere called Daath). The connection – both energetically and sexually – between the throat and the genitals is well-known, and can lead to the clearer expression of spirituality on the mundane plane of Malkuth.

We only speak of 'levels' of energy for convenience and so our usual linear language can at least approximately describe the actual multi-dimensional experience. Workers in the field of healing know from their experience that if they affect one level of energy, this effect will carry through to other levels. In practice, therefore, if we can change our relationship to energies in the third world of Yetzirah, this healing will be transmitted through to the other worlds. This is the reason why visualization, for instance, can be so powerful a healing tool. It works directly on the astral level, but any changes that occur there are mirrored on the etheric level, which then directly affect the physical world.

Similarly, if we work directly on the physical plane we can effect change on the subtler planes of energy. The different levels of energy are really more clearly understood as a continuum that connects the densest physical world with the subtlest spiritual realms. If we 'dance until we drop' as suggested in the chapter on 'Ways of Action', we are affecting our subtle energies through direct physical action. If we meditate and pray as suggested in the last chapter, 'Ways of Stillness', we may directly affect our physical world through indirect, inner processes. However we effect a healing, though, it is most important that we are aware of this continuum of energy which not only links all our different levels of energy but also connects us to everyone and everything else. This knowledge gives us an awesome connection to the deepest sources of energy and also the attendant responsibilities. If we use our inner understanding wisely, we realize all our actions affect the whole, and may effect a 'whole healing' as discussed above, not only on a personal but also on interpersonal and collective levels.

CONTACT WITH 'EXTRA-DIMENSIONAL' BEINGS

All cultures throughout our planet's history have described beings and creatures that exist in other realities or dimensions in parallel with and sometimes interpenetrating our world. In the view of some mainstream psychologists, these 'extra-dimensional' beings are the impersonal forces of nature which we personalize so we can attempt to gain control over them. According to some more far-sighted psychologists and those aware of the work of the new physics, however, these beings are representational of real forces. Looked at superficially, our world is composed of atoms and molecules which arrange themselves to create the different life forms we directly perceive. If we examine this basic atomic reality under an electron microscope, we enter the world of sub-atomic particles. This is a level of existence where different laws apply, but it is no less real simply because we cannot see it on a mundane level. The same applies to the 'levels of existence' which we cannot perceive with our usual senses but which are, despite this, no less real.

As our work with the Qabalah progresses and we wish to use the Tree of Life for our healing, we start to meet 'other beings'. At first sight this may appear strange, even ridiculous, until we consider the nature of these 'extra-dimensional' beings. Any being or entity outside of ourselves can be considered this way, including other human beings. Whether these 'beings' actually exist outside or whether they are figments of our imagination, projections, or parts of us that we do not recognize as being part of us, we all have the experience that they exist.

All the beings that inhabit our world, including animals, plants and all living and so-called non-living things, are apparently outside of us and we meet with them primarily in Malkuth. At a deeper level we meet 'astral' entities that inhabit the lower spheres on the Tree. These 'astral beings' include those we meet in dreams, astral projections, fantasies, visualization, and include all symbols and thought-forms. Tiphareth, whilst primarily associated with our own essential selves, is also the sphere for contact with our Guardian Angels. Whether these Angels exist outside of us matters little in practical terms; when we contact Tiphareth we find such beings in attendance. Then on even deeper levels of the Tree we may 'contact' Archangels and, if we reach the Supernal Triad, we may have contact with the Deity or some aspect of it.

Daath is the unnumbered sphere that resides in the Abyss between the Supernal Triad and the lower Tree. It is said to be the access point to the reverse side of the Tree where all the demons that bring 'dis-ease' into our lives exist. Again whether these 'demons' merely represent aspects of our own shadow nature and inhabit the dark recesses of our being, or whether they are actual entities with a life of their own, is an irrelevant issue. We can communicate with them and affect our relationship with them *as if* they are real.

The question arises why anyone would want to make contact with astral entities, Archangels or any other 'being' of this type, particularly demons! To answer this question we have to return to our definition of healing as making something whole. If we are to be whole, to include rather than exclude all our energies, one way of achieving this is through making contact with all the forces within our universe. We are usually quite willing to include the 'good guys' – if I suggest that you talk to your Guardian Angel you would probably have little resistance (assuming you believed it possible). On the other hand, once we discuss communicating with demons we are entering the realm of the shadow which includes those parts of ourselves that we would rather not face.

Any aspect of our being and our energy that we exclude from our awareness becomes part of our shadow which has been usefully described as being like a big bag we drag round behind us. The more shadow we have, the more we are excluding, the heavier our bag becomes and the more it restricts our free movement. Conversely, the more material from this 'shadow bag' we can dredge out, face, deal with, and integrate into our conscious being, the lighter the bag becomes and the more energy we have available to fulfil our life functions, from the loftiest sense of Divine Purpose through to the everyday functions that help us survive in the world.

If we do not face our anger over, say, a poor work situation, this suppressed anger and the associated anxiety will become part of our shadow. If we find ways of facing and expressing the anger, we will no longer be pulled down by the weight of it, and will free our energies, perhaps to make a life-enhancing decision about the work. On the other hand, if we do not express our anger, it will get pushed deeper and deeper down into the shadow bag until we are no longer even aware of its existence. As a result there will be tension and holding patterns in our body which will cause pain and disease later in life. We might start smoking tobacco to alleviate the stress from denying the anger; we might over-eat in an attempt to suppress the attendant feelings.

We can then say that our behaviour opens us up to the influence of the corresponding demonic force. For instance, a demon whose presence brings 'cancerous misgrowth of cells' might be allowed a foothold in the physical body, and lead to severe illness and death. We do not have to believe in demons to understand the process of what is happening. Perhaps what we are dealing with is a personification of the suppressed material in an individual's subconscious. Whatever we believe, however, what we can do is to encourage this person to start communicating with their demons or 'suppressed energies', find what they need to express, and through various appropriate actions, dispel the demons through releasing the pent-up anger. Thus we can heal through 'communicating with demons'.

There are many ways of using the Qabalah for healing, working with 'demons' being just one of them. The following tables detail the different parts of the body as they are attributed to the Tree. The disorders and diseases typical for each sphere or path on the Tree can be deduced easily from these tables. For example, if there was a disorder or disease originating in your liver (jaundice perhaps), it would show that the demons of the associated path (that from Tiphareth to Hod) were affecting your being. If you had a stomach ulcer it may suggest that a problem was occurring on the path joining Tiphareth to Netzach which was allowing the attendant 'negative' energies (or demons) to manifest in this way.

THE CENTRAL NERVOUS SYSTEM

Functions: Experience, response, communication and integration. Expression of life principles, ideals, purpose, revelation
Associated energy centres: Crown and mid-head chakras
Body parts: Head and back

Tree of Life	Human Body
Kether	life energy, 'consciousness'
Chockmah	brain – left hemisphere
Binah	brain – right hemisphere
path joins 1–2	left eye, ear, pituitary
path joins 1–3	right eye, ear, pineal
path joins 2–3	nose, mouth
path joins 1–6	spinal cord
path joins 6–9	spinal cord, (solar plexus)

THE ENDOCRINE SYSTEM

Functions: Energy and growth
Survival and expression
Associated energy centre: Throat chakra
Body parts: Neck, shoulders and arms, endocrine system

Tree of Life	Human Body
Chesed	left adrenal
Geburah	right adrenal
Daath	throat, thyroid
path joins 2–4	posterior pituitary and overall system
path joins 3–5	anterior pituitary and overall system

THE CARDIO-VASCULAR AND RESPIRATORY SYSTEMS

Functions: Energy exchange, quality of life, defence and transport
Transformation and love
Associated energy centre: Heart chakra
Body parts: Thorax

Tree of Life	Human Body
Tiphareth	heart, thymus
path joins 2–6	arteries, oxygenated blood
path joins 3–6	veins, de-oxygenated blood

path joins 4–5	lymph, spleen
path joins 4–6	left lung
path joins 5–6	right lung

THE DIGESTIVE AND EXCRETORY SYSTEMS

Functions: Ingestion, digestion, absorption, discrimination and elimination
Processing and clearing of desires
Associated energy centre: Solar Plexus chakra
Body parts: Abdomen

Tree of Life	*Human Body*
Netzach	left kidney
Hod	right kidney
path joins 4–7	large intestine (descending), rectum
path joins 6–7	stomach
path joins 5–8	large intestine (ascending and transverse)
path joins 6–8	liver, gall bladder, pancreas
path joins 7–8	small intestines
path joins 9–10	bladder, skin

THE REPRODUCTIVE SYSTEM

Functions: Connection, propagation, balance
Manifestation of energies
Associated energy centre: Sacral chakra
Body parts: Inner and outer sexual organs

Tree of Life	*Human Body*
Yesod	sexual organs
path joins 7–9	male: left seminal vesicle, vas deferens
	female: left hand uterine tube, ovaries
path joins 8–9	male: right seminal vesicle, vas deferens
	female: right uterine tube, ovaries

THE LOCOMOTOR SYSTEM

Functions: Support, movement, expression.
Grounding, will-to-live (hereditary, genetic, cultural influences)
Associated energy centre: Base chakra
Body parts: Legs, feet, skeletal and muscular systems

Tree of Life	Human Body
Malkuth	body as whole
path joins 7–10	left skeleton, bones, muscles
path joins 8–10	right skeleton, bones, muscles

It is said that the demonic forces use your physical vehicle to come through into manifestation on the Tree of Life. One way of dealing with the resultant disorders and diseases is through contacting the appropriate positive force to counteract the intrusion of the demons. Thus, for instance, if the disease was associated with Hod (relating to the right kidney), the use of the positive attributes of this sphere will counteract the disease. If we wished to counteract a disease in Hod, we may wear the appropriate colour (orange) next to the diseased place, chant the name and invoke the corresponding deity (Elohim Tzabaoth), fill the room with the corresponding flowers, concentrate on relevant animals and gemstones – using all the correspondences to this part of the Tree of Life to bring more of the positive aspect of the path into the field of consciousness of the diseased person.

HEALING WITH THE TREE

As I have shown, there are many different ways of healing with the Tree of Life. Already discussed are psychological approaches to wholeness as a form of healing, the Qabalistic attitude to sexual healing, and healing through contacting and transforming our relationship to our 'demons'. It is important to stress that the best healing is the one we

111

perform on ourselves. The old adage, 'healer, heal thyself' is most important. We have to be in the process of healing our own wounds before we are able to connect with, let alone heal, the wounds of others. This does not mean we have to be 'perfect' in some way before we can heal, but it is important that healing ourselves becomes a continuing process.

Whenever we do some personal healing on ourselves, we inevitably bring more health to the planet as a whole. Each little bit of increased consciousness adds to the total pool of consciousness available to all creatures. Our good acts 'live after us' – and so, unfortunately, do our 'bad acts'. If we are able to bring more wholeness into our lives, consciously and with good intention, we add to the total amount of 'wholeness' present on the earth. So Qabalistic healing is not only for us or for other individuals, but for everyone. This responsibility should not be overlooked when we wish to undertake any acts of healing, however insignificant they may seem.

In the following exercise we will be looking at how, through connecting to the Tree of Life, we can bring some healing energy into our own sphere of existence. It focuses particularly on the Middle Pillar. The spheres on the Tree of Life correspond to energy centres on the human body as shown in diagram 8. Through finding their correspondence in our own bodies, we can use all the associated images and symbols to effect our healing. The exercise is intended as a simple introduction to this work and it is not advised you apply this knowledge to working with others, or for more deeply working on yourself, without further guidance and a thorough grounding in the Tree of Life. If you are interested in taking this subject, or any other aspects of the practical Qabalah further, there is advice in the Afterword.

Exercise 9: The Healing Tree

Find a comfortable place where you can sit or lie in a relaxed fashion but without falling asleep. Spend at least five minutes focusing on your breathing. Do not force it or change it in any way, but keep to your own rhythm.

Now deepen your breathing a little and connect your out-breath with your in-breath. This means that once you have finished breathing out, immediately start breathing in and once you have completed an in-breath, immediately breathe out. This connected breathing process is very easy to do yet very powerful.

Focus on yourself as a Tree of Life (see diagram 8), overlaying the image of the Tree on your body.

Concentrate particularly on the middle Pillar of Kether, Daath, Tiphareth, Yesod and Malkuth. Kether (the Crown) is at the very top of your head, Daath (Knowledge) is at the level of the throat, Tiphareth (Beauty) at the heart, Yesod (Foundation) the lower belly and Malkuth (the Kingdom) at the base of your spine. Move between the top and bottom of the Tree as it corresponds to your body, attempting as much as possible to get the whole picture.

As you breathe in, focus your attention on energy rising up the Middle Pillar, up the back of your body. As you breathe out, focus your attention on energy coming down the Middle Pillar and down the front of your body. Keeping your breathing connected as before, let this cycle of energy build up within you.

Determine where energy is needed in you to restore balance. You may already be aware of this place in your body, or you may like to simply ask yourself the question: where do I need healing?

Give yourself over to this place in your body, visualizing energy there. On your in-breath imagine the energy there becomes stronger and more balanced, on your out-breath that you let out all dis-ease and unbalance.

Allow yourself to relax in this place in your body and let go of all the tension.

See if there is a colour or image that will aid your balance and simply imagine this colour or image sinking into this part of your body. Keep this up, letting the part of your body with which you are working be filled with the energy of the colour or image.

Now focus on your breathing again, directing your attention from this place in your body and returning to the image of the Middle Pillar of the Tree of Life, then the whole Tree.

Take some time to be aware of your whole body, relaxed, feeling well and 'healed'.

Return to your normal waking consciousness and, in whatever way feels appropriate to you, thank the forces which have aided this healing process within your body. Affirm that your healing is part of the healing of the whole of life on our planet and beyond.

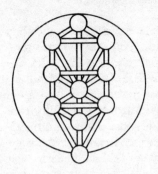

10 · THE HEART OF THE TREE

These six the adept harmonized, and said: this is the heart of the One and the All.

Aleister Crowley

At the centre of the Tree of Life is the sphere numbered six and called Tiphareth which corresponds with the centre of each individual being. This 'centre' is given numerous different names, many of which are used by different people in different ways. For example, Tiphareth relates to the 'ego' in one sense of that word but not in another. If we say Tiphareth is equivalent to the 'soul' some Qabalists would agree, others would argue vehemently. As the sphere of our innermost identity, however, whatever it is called, Tiphareth always remains a mystery that can only be truly understood through direct experience.

The easiest way to describe Tiphareth is to say it is the sphere of *pure self awareness*, or quite simply, the 'I'. This is the 'I' that has a personality consisting of Netzach (feelings), Hod (thoughts), Yesod (subconscious instincts and desires) and Malkuth (senses and body). Whatever 'pure self awareness' means to us as a concept is not what is meant, for Tiphareth transcends all intellectual understanding. As soon as we describe the experience of Tiphareth we are on shaky ground for it is beyond all words. To communicate something of its

115

'flavour', however, is not difficult, and the exercise at the end of this chapter offers you the opportunity to experience what Tiphareth is for yourself.

Tiphareth means 'Beauty' and 'Harmony', the beauty created when everything is synthesized into a complete whole, the harmony that results from living life from a clearly defined centre. Tiphareth is attributed to both the sun (at the centre of our solar system) and the heart (at the 'centre' of our human system). A correlation is thus made between the sun and the heart and this can help us understand the energy described by this sphere. To put it quite simply, the sun can be described as the point in the solar system around which everything else clusters or revolves. Similarly, the heart can be described as having this position in the human system.

As already mentioned in Chapter 1, from our position on the earth we see the sun as being born each morning, rising to a peak, descending again, then dying at the end of the day, to be (hopefully) reborn again the next day. Of course with our modern scientific knowledge we 'know' that this is not a 'true' perception, that the earth revolves and the sun is always there, it is just that some of the time we are on the wrong side of the planet to see it. But in terms of our direct experience, we are no different from our ancestors who did not have this scientific knowledge. We see the sun rise, we see the sun set, and we most definitely know it is not there during the night!

If we could step from the earth and stand on the sun (without being burnt up), our direct experience would change. We would see that the light of the sun is continuous, always shining, and that all the planets, asteroids, moons and other material that make up the solar system continually revolve around us. We could be said then to have changed our view from a terrestrial to a solar perspective.

Similarly, in our ordinary 'earthly' existence, we experience ourselves (and all other beings) as being born, growing, declining, then dying. If we happen to believe in an after-life or reincarnation, we will believe there is something after death, but our direct experience is that people are born, they live, they die and then they are no more. If we could step out of our 'earth consciousness' and into 'solar consciousness', our perspective would change as it did when we imaginatively stepped onto the sun. Now we would see that whilst individual manifested beings with physical bodies and personalities come and go, there is something that remains constant, a light that continues to shine. This 'light' is the soul or pure self awareness as represented on the Tree of Life by Tiphareth. Everything inevitably changes all the time, but the solar 'I' remains omniscient, omnipotent and omnipresent.

When we are living within our personalities (as represented by all the spheres below Tiphareth) we are attached to or identified with the contents of our awareness. We are sensing, feeling, thinking or some combination thereof. If we are angry, for instance, we do not see it as something we have, we act as if it is something we are. Different people tend to make different attachments in their personalities. Some are more identified with their thoughts and look upon Hod as the central pivot of their existence. Others are more identified with their feelings and look upon Netzach as the experience of most importance in life. There is nothing 'wrong' with being identified in this way. It is, in fact, absolutely essential, enabling us to experience the world and express ourselves. We also need, however, the ability to withdraw from these attachments altogether, and to be in a clear space, dis-identified from our personalities. From this clear space it is then possible to make a choice to re-attach as seems appropriate. Tiphareth (the sun and the heart) is the place where this clarity may be experienced. The Virtue traditionally associated with this sphere is called 'Devotion to the Great Work'. This Great Work is what was succinctly described by Jesus as 'Know Thyself'. It is through contacting Tiphareth and realizing our heart energy in everyday life that we can truly know ourselves and perform this Great Work.

THE SPIRIT AND THE SPARK

In an earlier chapter we described Kether, at the top of the Tree of Life, as being the Universal Spirit that is common to everyone and everything. Tiphareth is then seen as the spark of that Spirit that can be found at the heart or centre of each individual. For each of us it is our individualized bit of Spirit and, as such, can be related to the individual soul. In other words, Tiphareth is the personal self, the self-aware 'I' which is a reflection of the Spiritual Self into human consciousness. Another way of describing this is to say that the Universal Spirit projects a small portion of self-consciousness, Tiphareth, which may grow in self awareness, intelligence, the power to act, and so on. This growth will proceed most effectively under the combined nourishment of energies coming directly from the Spirit and those from the fertile soil of an earthly existence.

The paths that converge on Tiphareth from higher up the Tree of Life bring energies or 'Qualities' such as Love, Joy, Truth, Beauty, Courage, Freedom and Wonder, to each individual being. Whilst the overall quantity of these energies is the same for all of us, we each have a different combination of these Qualities with which to work in our life. These Qualities, similar to Archetypes, flow through Tiphareth into the personality and then become diffused into everyday experience.

It is obviously in our interests to connect more clearly and thoroughly with these Qualities so they can have more expression in our lives. One way of strengthening their flow is through contact with Tiphareth. Thus it is vitally important that we learn to dis-identify from our personalities and build a strong centre. Of equal importance, however, is the need to work actively on clarifying our personalities. We can then become better 'receptacles' or 'containers' for these Spiritual Qualities and become more able to express them for our own good and the good of our planet. We then connect back to Malkuth, the earth, without which our work remains ungrounded and, from the point-of-view of active service for the planet, worthless.

HEART ENERGY

If we look again at diagram 8, the Tree of Life overlaid on a human body, we see that Tiphareth corresponds to the position of the heart in the centre of the chest. Physically our hearts may be slightly off centre, but energetically speaking our hearts are right in the middle. Both Eastern and Western systems of understanding the energies of the physical body agree on this. The 'anahata' or heart centre of the Eastern chakra system corresponds directly to Tiphareth.

To understand the working of this heart energy within our human bodies, we need to understand that Tiphareth has a dual aspect 'hidden behind it'. This dual aspect is represented on the Tree of Life by Geburah and Chesed which relate to the Archetypes of Will and Love respectively. The heart centre is, therefore, in reality a trinity. For this reason, for the heart centre to be truly open in an individual, there has to be a balance of Love and Will. Other energy centres may open partially or in a distorted way. The heart centre, however, is more of an 'on-off' affair: it is open if there is balanced energy between Chesed and Geburah, closed if there is not.

If the heart is totally closed and never opens it stops the free passage of energy through Tiphareth and will eventually lead to heart-death through becoming clogged up or blocked. If the heart remains open all the time, never able to close even when appropriate, it will eventually lead to heart-death from too much energy being channelled there, usually experienced as a heart attack. A connected and effective heart centre chooses to open or close as appropriate to the situation at hand, being able to heal itself and others, but also able to protect its body from unwanted intrusions.

The heart is associated with 'higher' feelings such as altruistic love and compassion. Given the current state of our planet, and given the dangers from having an imbalance at this level of energy, it is vital we learn to respect our hearts and live our lives from this clearer space. When we connect with our heart energy, we express ourselves with greater understanding and harmony and are able to 'speak from the heart'. We become more able to manifest our creative potential for wholeness, using this energy to heal ourselves, other people and our relationship with our environment. We bring love back into our vision of the planet and our purpose for being here. We learn that when we truly accept who we are, we can experience and express our inner wisdom. When we 're-member' our hearts in this way, and connect with

Tiphareth, our own fulfilment fosters the well-being of our planet.

When we connect with our heart energy, when we are working on our personal and spiritual development, we are adding to the total pool of consciousness around our planet. If we are aware of this process, we can see that, in essence, by doing this work we are manifesting love. Love is the energy that divides us but only so that we can have the opportunity of coming together again to experience the joy of union. We are born out of an undifferentiated unity – we are one with everything but, because we are one, we cannot experience it. As we grow and develop in life we become more and more differentiated, we become more unique and individual, more ourselves.

From this differentiated position we are able to experience love, for we are able to join with other people and other beings. Of course this includes sexual union, but it also includes all the other ways in which we can join harmoniously with others, whether for brief, passing moments or for lifetimes. Alive on our planet earth, we are all developing on the same Tree of Life. Every conscious act of love increases the chances of us reaching our common goal, the manifestation of peace and joy.

We are divided for the sake of love and when we realize this we can honour both our separateness and our moments of togetherness. This is true self-love, when we accept ourselves for who and what we are without complaint or criticism. This is, in fact, the only place from where we can truly grow and realize our own unique purpose for incarnation. Paradoxically, accepting the truth of who and what we are does not stop us from growing but instead accelerates our development until we can echo the words of a great Qabalist from the past: 'I and the Mother-Father Deity are One'.

Exercise 10: Solar Consciousness

This exercise offers you a simple and effective way of connecting with Tiphareth, the centre of pure self awareness and 'solar consciousness' at the heart of the Tree of Life. It is a particularly important exercise, so please only practise it with the right attitude and in the right space.

Sit upright, relaxed but attentive, and pay attention to your breathing without altering it or forcing it in any way. Spend a few minutes watching how the air flows in and out of your body in a natural, easy way.

Be aware of what is going on inside your body. Be as fully aware of your body as you are able to be.

Ask yourself: Who is aware of my breathing? Who is aware of my body? Who is aware?

Now imagine a sphere around this body awareness and that you step back out of it. Vividly imagine in front of you a sphere that contains your body awareness. It is called Malkuth.

Consider your feelings. Are you feeling happy, sad, or what? Spend some time looking at your feelings.

How do you feel? Be aware of how your feelings change all the time. For instance, you may be sad one minute, happy the next. Be as fully aware of your feelings as you are able. Ask yourself: Who is aware of my feelings?

Now imagine a sphere around this feeling awareness and that you step back out of it. Vividly imagine in front of you a sphere that contains your awareness of feelings. It is called Netzach.

Consider your thoughts. What are you thinking right now? You are probably thinking about this exercise, but what other thoughts are coming in and out of your awareness? Watch the flow of these thoughts for a while without getting caught up in them.

Your thoughts come and go almost as if they are independent of you. Be as fully aware of your thought processes as you are able. Ask yourself: Who has these thoughts?

Now imagine a sphere around your thoughts and that you step back out of it. Vividly imagine in front of you a sphere that contains your awareness of thoughts. It is called Hod.

Focus on these three spheres of awareness, your sensations in Malkuth, feelings in Netzach, thoughts in Hod. Who is focusing on these spheres?

Ask yourself: Who am I? Who is it that experiences all these sensations, feelings, thoughts?

Allow yourself to experience fully this part of you that has sensations, feelings and thoughts but is more than any or all of them. This is solar consciousness, the experience of Tiphareth.

Be aware of yourself as a unique being with pure self awareness.

You can choose to be separate or non-attached to the contents of your personality. You can also choose to go into any of these spheres of awareness when it is appropriate for you to do so. Choose now to re-enter your personality and take some time to bring yourself back into everyday consciousness. You can do this through concretely expressing your connection to Tiphareth. What do you wish to do to express clearly your connection to your heart?

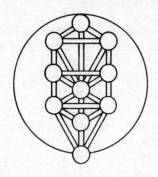

AFTERWORD

I hope you have enjoyed reading this book and learning about the Qabalah and the Tree of Life. One of the most exciting aspects of the Qabalah is that the more you use it, the more interesting and useful it becomes. As you delve further into practical Qabalistic work, the Tree of Life becomes alive in your consciousness. It lives with you in everything you do: increasing your awareness, deepening your connection to soul energy, giving you assistance in manifesting who you are and what you want to be in life. Only practical experience can show you the true value of the Qabalah.

After reading this book you may think the Qabalah is not for you or that it is an interesting path but not one you choose at this time. The Qabalah is definitely of little value to someone unless they feel personally connected to it. On the other hand, having found something here to interest you, you may wish to continue your study and practice of the Qabalah:

1. simply to know more about it so you can decide whether you wish to go further into its mysteries and revelations;

2. to foster your individual growth and development;

3. to add new skills, and develop your work in whatever field that may be;

4. to become a Qabalist, using the Tree of Life as a major tool in your path towards Self-realization.

It is possible to make Qabalah a dry, intellectual study and if that is what you desire and enjoy all well and good. I would like to stress again, however, the importance of practice. Without it, you will be missing the excitement and meaning that is found when the Tree of Life shines in your everyday life and lights up the path towards your goals whatever they may be. The Qabalah is of equal value for those travelling the simplest, most mundane path as it is for those attempting the loftiest peaks of attainment. The practical Qabalah is for *everyone* who wishes to partake of its splendours.

A lot can be gleaned from reading books on the Qabalah and related subjects, particularly those books which offer you practical suggestions and exercises. Reading is best accompanied by experiences so that you can connect what you read with your own personal process. The books in Further Reading are a good place to start with this work. *The Living Qabalah* is an excellent practical guide to Qabalistic theory and practice. It encapsulates twenty years of practical work with the Tree of Life.

There are an increasing number of people who either teach Qabalah or share their insights about the Qabalah with others. I would suggest that if you decide to attend or join any on-going groups, you do not make a commitment until you have experienced what they offer. Anyone who asks you to do otherwise is probably to be avoided. Be wary also of any group leaders who ask you to follow their teachings or practices to the exclusion of your reading other books or following any other course of study that interests you. The Qabalah is not intended to be an exclusive system – indeed, part of its value is its ability to interrelate with other systems.

I offer individual tuition in the Qabalah, basing the work on your own life experience and needs, not through applying a set formula without regard to who you are. I also run day and weekend groups on Qabalah and related subjects. If you would like details of these ventures please feel free to write to me care of the publisher.

Whatever your feelings about the Qabalah, may your search for inner wisdom and understanding be fruitful, and may you come to a self-realization that nurtures both your own individual experience and expression and that of the planet as a whole.

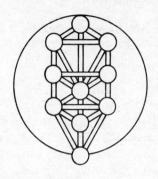

APPENDIX 1: THE SACRED ALPHABET

Each Hebrew letter is a symbolic representation of a cosmic principle and has a specific meaning and a number attributed to it. This is explained in more detail in Chapter 4.

There are twenty-two letters in the Hebrew alphabet and they are related to the twenty-two paths on the Tree of Life. They represent different states of consciousness that are created when the cosmic principles represented by the spheres are connected through human awareness. The letters then represent the essence or principle behind these connections.

The following table shows the Hebrew letters and some of their major correspondences. For more detailed tables see *The Living Qabalah* (Further Reading).

THE ELEMENTS OF THE QABALAH

Hebrew letter	Hebrew name	English equivalent	Numerical value	English letters	Attribution	Path on Tree of Life
א	aleph	ox	1	A	air	joins 1–2
ב	beth	house	2	B	mercury	joins 1–3
ג	gimel	camel	3	C, G	moon	joins 1–6
ד	daleth	door	4	D	venus	joins 2–3
ה	he	window	5	H	aquarius	joins 2–6
ו	vau	nail	6	U, V	taurus	joins 2–4
ז	zain	sword	7	Z	gemini	joins 3–6
ח	cheth	fence	8	Ch	cancer	joins 3–5
ט	teth	serpent	9	T	leo	joins 4–5
י	yod	hand	10	I, Y	virgo	joins 4–6
כ	kaph	palm	20	K	jupiter	joins 4–7
ל	lamed	ox-goad	30	L	libra	joins 5–6
מ	mem	water	40	M	water	joins 5–8
נ	nun	fish	50	N	scorpio	joins 6–7
ס	samekh	support	60	S	sagittarius	joins 6–9
ע	ayin	eye	70	O	capricorn	joins 6–8
פ	pe	mouth	80	P	mars	joins 7–8
צ	tzaddi	fish-hook	90	X, Tz	aries	joins 7–9
ק	qoph	backhead	100	Q	pisces	joins 7–10
ר	resh	head	200	R	sun	joins 8–9
ש	shin	tooth	300	Sh	fire/spirit	joins 8–10
ת	tau	cross	400	Th	saturn/earth	joins 9–10

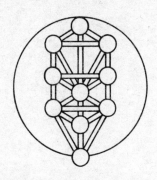

APPENDIX 2: STANDARD SYMBOLS

The symbols used in this book are fairly standard. They are:

PLANETS

Earth ⊗	Sun ☉	Moon ☽	Mercury ☿
Venus ♀	Mars ♂	Jupiter ♃	Saturn ♄
Uranus ♅	Neptune ♆	Pluto ♇	

ELEMENTS

Fire △	Water ▽	Air △	Earth ▽

ZODIAC

Aries ♈	Taurus ♉	Gemini ♊	Cancer ♋
Leo ♌	Virgo ♍	Libra ♎	Scorpio ♏
Sagittarius ♐	Capricorn ♑	Aquarius ♒	Pisces ♓

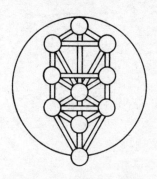

FURTHER READING

The following books are recommended further reading for those of you who wish to continue your studies of the practical Qabalah. You will obtain most understanding from those described as 'essential study'. All the other listed titles contain some Qabalistic knowledge and are also highly recommended.

1. ESSENTIAL STUDY OF PRACTICAL QABALAH

Fortune, D. *The Mystical Qabalah*, Benn, 1970 [a classic if somewhat dated text].
Gonzalez-Wippler, M. *A Kabbalah For The Modern World*, Llewellyn, 1987 [first class rendition of Qabalistic understanding].
Hoffman, E. *The Way of Splendour*, Shambhala, 1981 [modern Qabalah from an enlightened Jewish viewpoint].
Parfitt, W. *The Living Qabalah*, Element, 1988 [essential for study of the practical Qabalah].

2. OTHER RECOMMENDED PRACTICAL QABALAH TEXTS

Andrews, T. *Imagick*, Llewellyn, 1989.
Crowley, A. *The Qabalah of Aleister Crowley* (inc: 777), Weiser, 1973.
Halevi, Z. *The Work of the Kabbalist*, Gateway, 1984.
Knight, G. *Practical Guide to Qabalistic Symbolism*, Weiser, 1978.

Love, J. *Quantum Gods*, Element, 1976.

Regardie, I. *The Tree of Life*, Weiser, 1972.

Schaya, L. *The Universal Meaning of the Kabbalah*, Penguin USA, 1974.

Scholem, G. *On The Kabbalah*, Schochen, 1965.

3. BOOKS ON MAGICK, TAROT AND ASSOCIATED SUBJECTS:

Alli, A. *Angel Tech*, Falcon, 1986.

Casteneda, C. *Tales of Power*, Penguin, 1976.

Crowley, A. *The Book of Thoth*, Weiser, 1971.

Crowley, A. *Magick*, Weiser, 1973.

Crowley, A. and Harris, F. *The Thoth Tarot Cards*, Various editions. [By far the best Qabalistic tarot cards, and also very beautiful in design. Highly recommended.]

Goodison, L. *Moving Heaven & Earth*, Womens Press, 1990.

Greer, M. *Tarot Transformation*, Aquarian, 1984.

Parfitt, W. *Walking Through Walls*, Element, 1989.

Regardie, I. *The Complete Golden Dawn*, Falcon, 1984.

Starhawk, *The Spiral Dance*, Harper & Row, 1979.

Wanless, J. *New Age Tarot*, Merrill-West, 1987.

Wilson, R. *Prometheus Rising*, Falcon, 1983.

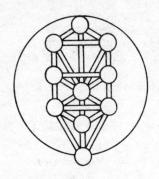

GLOSSARY

Abyss The gulf between the phenomenal world of manifestation (Chesed and below) and its noumenal source (the Supernal Triad). Only through crossing the Abyss can we realize our innermost spiritual nature.

Adam Man, literally 'red earth' or 'first blood'. 'Adam Kadmon' is the prototype of all human creatures (male and female).

Adonai Lord, the personal 'deity within', or the Holy Guardian Angel (of which each manifest creature has at least one).

Ain Nothing, the void.

Ain Soph The energy through which nothing becomes something. The primal creative energy.

Ain Soph Aur Limitless Light, the void beyond the known universe represented by the Tree of Life.

Assiah The fourth world of material manifestation, of humans and other manifest beings.

Atziluth The first world of creative essence, the realm of the Mother-Father Deity.

Barakah Grace, divine blessing bestowed when 'desire' and 'reality' are united.

Binah Understanding, the third sephirah, relating to Saturn. The first sphere beyond the abyss. (Sometimes erroneously called 'reason', a patriarchal misunderstanding.)

Briah The second world of receptive essence and pure spirit, the realm of Archangels.

Cabala see Qabalah

Chesed Mercy, Love, the fourth sephirah, relating to Jupiter.

Chockmah Wisdom, the second sephirah, relating to Neptune, the sphere associated with Spiritual Purpose.

Daath Knowledge, the 'eleventh' sephirah or 'the sphere without a number', the gateway to the 'hidden' Tree behind the visible one, relates to Uranus.

Eden The 'garden' of 'unity' to which we return when we realize divine 'union' here on earth.

Elohim Usually translated as 'God', the word is composed of a feminine singular with a masculine plural, thus expressing the uniting of male and female principles.

Eve The 'first woman'; the inner aspect of all humans (male and female) through which we come to know ourselves.

Geburah Strength, Judgement, the fifth sephirah, relating to Mars.

Gematria Qabalistic numerological system where words having the same numerical value are said to be essentially identical. A meditational and revelatory technique.

Great Work An alchemical term summarized in the words of Jesus: 'Know Thyself'.

Hod Splendour, the eighth sephirah, related to Mercury, the sphere of thinking.

Immanence Belief or experience that the divine is already manifest in all things and is to be found within. (c/f transcendence.) The Way of the Qabalah is essentially biased towards immanence.

Kabbalah see Qabalah.

Kavvanah Conscious meditation or prayer.

Kether Crown, the first sephirah, related to Pluto, transmits the influences from 'trans-mundane' realms.

Maggid Any trans-mundane entity with whom the Qabalist communicates; also a spiritually advanced human being.

Magick Any intentional act is an act of magick, which has been described as the art of causing willed change. A world-view which gives precedence to immanence rather than transcendence.

Malkuth Kingdom or Bride, the tenth sephirah, related to earth, the total manifestation of all matter.

Mysticism Any method designed to bring the practitioner closer to union with their higher Self is mystical. A world-view which gives precedence to transcendence rather than immanence.

Netzach Victory, the seventh sephirah, related to Venus, the sphere of feelings.

Qabalah To receive, and by implication also to reveal. A practical system for understanding ourselves and our relationship with our world.

Qliphoth The plural of 'qliphah' meaning 'shells' or 'otherness' (sometimes erroneously and patriarchally called 'woman'!), the shadow side of the sephiroth on the Tree of Life, the qliphoth are the realms of 'demons'.

Ruach Spirit. Patriarchally related to 'air' and 'reason'; originally – and correctly – related to 'water' and the womb out of which all life – male and female – appears.

Sephirah Number, Emanation, Sphere, Container. The name given to each of the eleven emanations of cosmic manifestation on the Tree of Life that underlie the whole of existence.

Sephiroth The plural of Sephirah.

Shekhinah The female embodiment of spiritual power.

Supernal Triad The three Sephiroth above the Abyss, therefore beyond material manifestation. The source of all creation.

Tarot The 'tarot' of anything is its spiritual essence, its connection with the wheel of manifestation. Particularly related to the seventy-eight images (or cards) of the tarot pack that act as a compendium of all human knowledge and understanding.

Tetragrammaton IHVH, the four-lettered name of the Deity commonly referred to as Jehovah. Tetragrammaton contains a complex formula relating to cosmic union and the manifestation of the elements. Only after the creation is fully manifest is the term IHVH used for 'God' in the Bible.

Tiphareth Beauty, the sixth and central Sephirah on the Tree of Life, related to the Sun, and to the central core or heart of each individual.

Transcendence Belief or experience that the divine is separate, not-manifest and is to be found through acts which separate us from mundane reality. (c/f immanence.)

Tree of Life The ten sephiroth and the twenty-two connecting paths. All forms – manifest, unmanifest, animate and inanimate – mirror this structure.

Yesod Foundation, the ninth sephirah, related to the Moon, astral and sexual energy. Also the place where unresolved subconscious material is 'deposited' in the individual and collective psyche.

Yetzirah The third world of formation, realm of Angels.

Zaddik A person who is well-versed in the path, a spiritual guide.

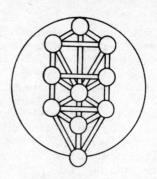

INDEX